Roy Wyatt

Also by Roy Wyatt

The Professional Security Officer-Agent
Life Lessons Revealed
Private Security Management (1st and 2nd Edition)
Dark Secret
For Teens and Young Adults
A Promise Kept

EVERYTHING NEEDED TO BECOME A

SECURITY

PROFESSIONAL

PROTECTORS OF PEOPLE, PROPERTY, AND SERVICES

Roy Wyatt

Security Professional

CreateSpace Independent Publishing Platform, North Charleston, SC

Wyatt, Roy, 2018-
    Security Professional - Roy Wyatt.
    ISBN ISBN-13: 978-1718715264   ISBN-10: 1718715269

Printed in the United States of America

EVERYTHING NEEDED TO BECOME A

SECURITY PROFESSIONAL

PROTECTORS OF PEOPLE, PROPERTY, AND SERVICES

Dedication

The author respectfully dedicates this book to his loving parents, Mrs. Mary and John Lee Wyatt. To his Mom, who never spoke a harmful word against anyone, and his dad, who instilled in him the desire to accomplish anything he chooses.

May the God of Abraham, Isaac, and Jacob receive his spirit and may he find peace under the eyes of the Creator.

Contents

Roy Wyatt

CHAPTER 4   Security Officer Training

CHAPTER 5   The Client

CHAPTER 6   Security Posts / Positions

CHAPTER 7   What Every Security Officer Need to Know

CHAPTER 8   Getting to the Next Level

CHAPTER 9   Sample Interview Questions and General Knowledge Examination

Roy Wyatt

ACKNOWLEDGMENTS

Writing a book is a monumental task. Although the author's name appears on the cover, it requires a collaborative effort of insightful, inspirational, and supportive personnel behind the scenes to make the undertaking a success. As I've learned over the years, a few significant accomplishments can never be completed alone; this book is no exception. Though it would be virtually impossible to list all the people who have influenced and inspired me to write Security Professional, I want to recognize a special few who helped make this book possible.

First, I must thank God for my gifts, talents, life experiences, inspiration, and creativity, which made this book a reality.

Thanks to my parents, whose unconditional love, unselfishness, and encouragement freed me to chart my own path and follow my dreams. As the years go by, my appreciation grows for the example they set and the wisdom they passed down.

Thank you to Mark Slockbower for allowing me to manage. He saw the potential and believed in me.

Thank you to Kris Slimmer for his many suggestions, observations, and insights during his time.

Thank you to Alvin and Mary Fountain, Virginia and Rosson Trice, who inspired me. They have always been there with their business knowledge, support, and wisdom.

Thanks to my second set of parents: Auntie Liz, Ann, and Mary Clark (Niece). You made all the difference, and I will forever be thankful.

Boundless thanks to the many Security Professionals who set the course for my idea of writing on the topic. You are and always will be the most valuable asset of any security provider.

Additional authors and businesses that contributed to this publication are:

- *Mike Robbins/Author* - ways to remain flexible www.Mike-Robbins.com
- *Chuck Gallozzi – www.personal-development.com*
- *Todd Smith/Author - Little Things matter: articles: Take initiative, Focus, Being Disciplined*
- *Alexander Kjerulf/Author –* www.positivesharing.com *little things matter / 10 reasons why complaining is toxic*
- *Advanced Protective Services, LLC – Private Security vs. Public Law Enforcement*

Roy Wyatt

INTRODUCTION

Working in the Security Industry, managing multiple contracts and dealing with a diverse group of security personnel, three things stick out that cannot be ignored and must become a priority in preparing officers. 1—The majority of turnover can be directly attributed to being ill-prepared. This unpreparedness culminates in public perception, lack of discipline, and poor judgment.

Media portrayal continues to be a considerable factor in perception. However, this perception is far from the norm. Of course, a few employees will always fit a negative stereotype. However, most security professionals are highly trained, have good customer service skills, and are committed and professional in carrying out their duties. 2: Regardless of compensation, companies, clients, customers, and the general public expect Security Officers to be professional. So the expectations are still the same whether you're being paid $8.00 an hour or $15.00 an hour. And 3: the need for a higher caliber of officer is constantly being sought. From a global standpoint, everything as we know it from 20 years ago has changed. You must be prepared for technology, people, communications, jobs, education, and most of all, standards of quality. As a result, security officers are constantly being trained in new procedures to prepare for the ever-changing jobs of tomorrow.

Every facet of society has evolved, and Security Officers must be prepared to meet those demands. For this reason, more *professional* Security Officers are needed to carry out the activities on the client's worksite. Security Officers must not only *look* the part, but also be able to articulate communication while making informed decisions regarding the best interest of the Company and the Client. They must be proficient at carrying out their duties and responsibilities, knowing when emergency assistance is needed or when creating an Incident Report is warranted, and knowing the difference is usually key.

Successful businesses rely heavily on retaining customers and referrals. Finances aren't the biggest factor, but mostly how comfortable and secure customers felt conducting business with the Client. Since Security is the face of many businesses, they must understand and possess a high degree of customer service, interpersonal, and communication skills.

Since the competition is always catching up, businesses constantly look for ways to enhance their products and services while minimizing costs. Security Officers must understand this while still providing the expected level of service and commitment. This, too, is prevalent in the Security Industry. Security companies also continually look for ways to enhance their services, such as higher-quality *security officers.*

Businesses understand that how the public sees them equates to dollars and cents. Since security officers are the face of many businesses, their professionalism cannot be underestimated. Their interaction is key to the customer's perception of the Client's business and services.

The media cannot take all the blame for the negative perception of Private Security. They can't be responsible when officers are seen sleeping on duty, have terrible appearances, and have poor customer service and communication skills. This is directly attributed to the officer and, ultimately, the security industry. Immaturity, insufficient training, bad judgment, and meager wages still plague the industry as well. Some things cannot be changed, but many things can. This is what this book is about.

I want to introduce and prepare you not only for what's expected from the security industry and clients but also for the mindset, skills, and abilities required on your part to be a professional security officer. The industry has a lot of officers, but not everyone is experienced. A higher caliber officer is constantly needed with the diversity of clients, procedures, duties, and expectations. So, anyone desiring a career in this industry must bring their best.

Your job doesn't determine professionalism, pay rate, or status. It comes from within. It encompasses your attitude and how you see circumstances that determine your behavior and/or response. <u>No professional Security Officer comes to work with a dirty, wrinkled uniform or sleeps on the job. It cannot be blamed on anyone except themselves.</u>

Every Security Officer must have three things if they want to succeed in the Security industry: good appearance, positive attitude, and great customer service skills. A lack of any one will disqualify you from being professional. These key traits make up the basic qualifications.

Security Professionals should challenge every Security Officer to be Professional. The security industry demands a high degree of discipline, focus, flexibility, customer service, dedication, and communication skills. As a result, simply doing your best is not always good enough and often falls short of the expected level of quality and commitment.

Why do you think security officers are portrayed so negatively in the media? It's Simple. It's because they're expected to be professional. If the unacceptable behavior were expected, it would not warrant as much as a head turn. But it's not. Like Police Officers, when their behavior violates expectations, it's publicized like everything else. This makes the entire industry look bad and discredits the professional officers.

As the economy grows, so will the need for more Security officers......Professionals! According to the *Growth and Development of the Security Industry*, the Private Security industry is rapidly growing. Currently, there are 2 million full-time security workers in the United States – far outnumbering police officers, and this number is expected to increase by 21% through 2020. So let's be ready. Let's get prepared. Not only does your job depend on it, but thousands of companies, customers, and the general public.

Chapter 1
PERSONAL ASSESSMENT

Learning objectives

After reading this chapter, you should be able to

- Determine if a career in Private Security is right for you.

- Define the importance of understanding yourself.

- Define why confidence is so important.

- Identity key characteristics of successful security professionals.

- Identify components of workplace stress.

PERSONAL ASSESSMENT

Chapter 1
PERSONAL ASSESSMENT

Each year, many people enter Private Security only to find out later they're not cut out for it or can't handle the challenges of being a Security Professional. This lack of self-awareness negatively impacts co-workers, clients, and the industry. ***But how does an individual know if he or she is ready for a career in Private Security?*** Is there a defining test, experience, or success level guaranteeing qualification?

No one-way fit all approach

Many hiring managers can attest - there is no *"one-way-fits-all" approach* in determining success in any position. Although typically, the best predictor of future performance is past performance, what if you're moving into Private Security for the first time, or to a new Security position? How do you know if a career in Private Security is right for you?

> Whatever you believe about yourself on the inside is what you will manifest on the outside.

> **First, it's important to remember that although someone else may think you're ready for a security position, doesn't mean you are. Unfortunately, not everyone is destined to be a Security Professional.**

Negative Perception

Many people's perceptions of the industry aren't what they should be. They often attribute Security Professional duties to media outlets that don't display the true characteristics, commitment, and job proficiency.

Instead, many are shown performing mundane, laid-back duties with no real threat of Security. Their jobs require very little education, skillset, or commitment, so almost anyone can perform them. But nothing can be further from the truth.

As with many jobs, what's seen from the outside rarely reflects the accurate picture. There are many jobs within this industry, all requiring a different set of qualifications, skillset, focus, and commitment. Depending on your job site (account), you will be required to bring the appropriate skill set and qualifications. But you don't need to reinvent the wheel. Several key characteristics are specific to most jobs. These personal characteristics are vital and have proven successful for Security Professionals over the years. To better gauge your effectiveness, it's essential to understand them from the beginning.

> Knowing yourself means respecting (but not attaching) your strengths and weaknesses, your passions and fears, your desires and dreams, your thoughts and feelings, your likes and dislikes, your tolerances and limitations
>
> -   *Jane (Habits for wellbeing)*

Before pursuing a position in Private Security, ask yourself these questions.

■ How Do You Feel About Yourself?

If we are true to ourselves, we reflect who we are in everything: our friends, hobbies, likes/dislikes, even our jobs. These things paint a picture of our inner self, including our most sacred thoughts and desires.

One area in life that stands out drastically and impacts how we view everything, including each other, is how we feel about ourselves. This impacts how we think, view, feel, and respond to individuals and circumstances more than we know or care to think.

For instance, what if you believe things are always working against you and possess a lack of enthusiasm? How will this attitude impact dealing with co-workers, clients, and customers?

In Private Security, demonstrating enthusiasm for the job is vital to your success, as well as that of your employees and the company. People feed off others' attitudes. This is especially important when informing, giving advice, and directing other actions, as many security professionals do daily.

Staying enthusiastic is a huge link in employees' responsibility. It will be very ineffective if you possess an *"everyone is against me"* attitude.

Remember, you don't need to be in the position of your dreams to feel good about your job. But it helps to be comfortable where you are and within yourself. This promotes a positive outlook expressed in your everyday life. If not, it may reflect in your quality of work and performance, and ultimately rub off on employees.

Enforcing policies and procedures, providing direction and guidance, receiving constructive criticism, and convincing leaders and co-workers of one's abilities require confidence.

Moreover, if you tend to crumble when confronted with negative feedback or opposition, Private Security may not be the right fit. Without confidence in yourself, your co-workers won't have confidence in you either.

■ How Do You Feel Towards The Private Security Industry?

With approximately 2 million full-time workers and still experiencing record growth rates, Private Security is one of the fastest-growing industries. But this industry has been tarnished. Meager wages, limited to no benefits, minimum training requirements, and high turnover rates still plague them.

Armed with this information, it's imperative for security professionals (new arrivals and seasoned employees) to have the correct mindset about the industry. These are contracted jobs, and client bill rates will always dictate security professionals' wages.

Having said that, Private Security has many jobs at various levels of employment that appeal to employees from all walks of life. From entry-level to managerial, accounting, IT, finance, and more, the opportunities are endless, and you're only as limited as you desire to be.

It's true that many positions support the above statistics. However, many don't. These statistics are derived from smaller security firms without the necessary capabilities, technology, and finances to improve this industry rating.

> **THINKABOUT IT**
> Why is it so important to understand yourself?

The ones that do (larger firms) are very competitive in market wages and provide the necessary training to perform jobs on client sites.

Employees who stay with their contracts are usually more satisfied than those who don't, even with their wages. Statistics only tell part of the story and should not deter anyone from entering the industry or staying, for those wanting and requiring more, opportunities do exist.

Understand that Security officers/guards are the business in this industry. Without them, there would be no business. There would also be no need for managers. The Industry states that most of these employees are underpaid, undertrained, and have little to no benefits. Still, they provide the labor for everyone to remain employed while performing jobs even in the harshest conditions.

> Many Private Security jobs require a lot of focus, dedication, and commitment.

Bottom line: Contracts require hourly employees work days when exempt employees (salary employees), and some professions off enjoying time with family and friends, including Holidays and inclement weather.

Don't judge the industry by what you hear or perceive about it. Many Private Security Jobs require a great deal of focus, dedication, and commitment.

■ Would You Be Able To Set a Good Example For The Team?

Setting the example is a must if Security officers want to gain the trust and respect of their leaders and co-workers, and every effort should be made to continually set a positive one. If Security professionals do this, it can change the perception of service clients, security companies, and the general public.

It's important for managers to practice what they preach. Being a manager doesn't mean you no longer have to follow the laws of the land. Rather than spending time away from the job or always under their boss's nose, a manager should be working with their team members.

> Appearance matters a great deal because one can often tell a lot about people by how they present themselves.

To a large extent, a Security Officer's performance will be reflected in the response and performance of their team members. Their performance will also be reflected in how others interact with them. By leading by example, co-workers may follow that example. But let standards slip, and sloppy behavior can spread and quickly become routine.

Security Officers cannot expect to be treated respectfully when they are frequently late, call off, or allow their personal lives to impact their work performance. To start on the right foot, here are some things Security Officers need to be aware of.

FIRST IMPRESSION:

It's important for security professionals to make good first impressions and not get caught up in trying to look good and act like they know it all. A security officer who gets off to a bad start can find it challenging to change other people opinions later. It's important not to let their position and/or authority go to their head.

APPEARANCE:

Although you may consider it a sad commentary on a superficial society, appearance matters more than you think. We "all" make assumptions based on appearance. A security officer reporting for duty whose appearance is not up to par has already lost the respect of their co-workers and leaders without them ever saying a word. Your appearance is a chance to be a role model. Security officers must be appropriately dressed and ready for work every day, just as their company uniform and appearance guidelines state.

BE ON TIME:

Security Officers should not have a history of lateness, tardiness's or call-offs. Their attendance should set a good example. When a Security Officer is scheduled to work, they must be on time. This is especially crucial if another officer is waiting to be relieved after their shift has ended. All Jobs start with attendance. Without good attendance, you will quickly lose the respect of your peers, co-workers, and leaders.

■ Can You Keep Your Personal Problems From Getting in the Way of Performing your Job?

The truth is, we all have personal issues we must deal with. They are all too common. You know when a customer snaps at you unfairly, when you have a sick child, when you're going through a divorce, or when you have an ailing parent who needs your attention.

At home, your reaction can be different. You may lash out at someone and start a shouting match, or leave and take a long walk, or go somewhere and hide. But at work things are different. While these issues are important, these behaviors do not matter. It can seriously

> Control your feelings – don't let them control you.

jeopardize your professional reputation and hinder productivity. You've got to find a way to separate work from your personal problems to maintain your professional reputation, reduce workplace disruptions, and get the job done.

There are ways to manage your feelings effectively. However, if you cannot effectively manage your feelings when dealing with people, Private security may not be for you. Additionally, not controlling your feelings may open the door for allegations of discrimination and harassment.

■ Are You Disciplined to do What is Needed?

The art of being disciplined involves performing acts when you don't necessarily feel like it, or when it's uncomfortable, but necessary to achieve objectives. Chances are, if you are considering a field in Private Security, you have probably already demonstrated discipline. You may have completed a complex job assignment, volunteered for additional credits, or graduated from college. If so, this shows discipline in sticking with a task and seeing it through even when it gets tough.

Being a security professional involves discipline in focusing on company policy and job standards so they can be followed consistently. This creates a sense of stability and accountability.

> Being a Security officer involves being disciplined in focusing on adhering to company policies and standards.

Adhering to Policy

All company policies and procedures must be followed. For instance: Employees are required to follow the company's dress policy, be on time, act accordingly, perform duties respectfully and courteously, have great customer service and interpersonal skills, know how to diffuse situations, set the example, etc., etc., etc.

These are just a few of many qualities and characteristics required of employees. The Company Handbook will be filled with them.

Other areas Security Officers show discipline includes ....

- Ensuring uniform and appearance standards are adhered to
- Not being late for duty
- Maintaining self-control
- Owning up to their mistakes
- Following direction given by Supervisors and leaders
- Avoiding the use of profane or sarcastic language
- Not falsifying documents
- Not cheating (taking a short cut) on procedures when alone

High Standards

Security Professionals should have high standards. They are the backbone of businesses. Customers come in contact with them and derive their overall perception of the company from them. Security Professionals are expected to look, act, be knowledgeable, and perform all functions in a knowledgeable, respectful, and professional manner. Even in the presence of adversity, Security officers are expected to perform—no exceptions!

■ Can You Receive Constructive Criticism?

No one enjoys being criticized. It's why mastering the art of constructive criticism is such a helpful skill to develop when dealing with other people. No matter who you are, you'll likely find yourself in a position where you'll need to receive feedback, whether in your personal or professional life. As a company employee, it's your responsibility to receive feedback about your work performance. The reputation of the client's business, the security company, and your job depend on it.

It's inevitable, but some employees' performance will be unacceptable, maybe yours. Unfortunately, communicating when and how something could have been done better is part of a Supervisor or Manager's job. They have the responsibility to coach employees so they can perform better **next time.**

Believe me when I say this: No Supervisor or manager likes administering criticism. They'd much rather avoid it if they could. However, it's part of their job and something that must be done.

> **Constructive criticism** is often the only way we learn about our weaknesses—without it, we can't improve. When we're defensive, instead of accepting and gracious, we run the risk of missing out on this important insight.
> Remember, <u>feedback's not easy to give</u> and it's certainly not easy to receive, but it'll help us now and in the long run.

Personalities, skill levels, and maturity will all play a major role in how people react to constructive criticism. A mature adult will not generally respond the way they did as adolescents.

Employees should not feel bad about a situation that can be improved, but many still do. Instead of seeing it as an area for improvement, they interpret it as a personal attack.

Private Security may not be for you if you're one of those individuals who cannot receive constructive criticism without feeling personally attacked. Whenever working for someone else, the company has a requirement on how things are to be performed. Whenever your performance falls below par, instructing how something can and should be done is not only part of their job but a requirement.

■ Can You Handle Pressure?

Like many professions, private security jobs can also be pressure-filled, so knowing you can handle pressure is essential. As a Security officer, you are expected to stay cool under pressure and not explode at others when the pressure is on, nor collapse into a useless heap when you need to perform.

Security officers must be able to assess a situation, organize themselves, stay focused, and get the job done during stressful times. Pressure may come from all angles—this will be normal.

Security Officers will likely contend with stress in the following areas:

Staying focused for extended periods of time

Constantly remaining vigilant

Giving direction

Handling Accidents and Incidents

Enforcing rules and protecting property

Constantly interacting with customers

If dealing with pressure isn't your thing, you might want to reconsider. Many security positions can be pressure-filled. Regardless of the pressure, security officers are expected to produce and deliver. The areas listed above are just a few – there will be plenty more. When they come up, you must deal with them.

Pressure is part of the job. And little pressure is okay at times. But be wary of excessive pressure or stress. It can oftentimes lead to problems mentally and physically. If you are stressed, think about what's happening in your life. Some of the most common causes of stress to watch out for are:

Identify some components of on the job stress.

- Lack of self-control
- Increased responsibility
- Job dissatisfaction
- Uncertainty about work roles
- Poor communication
- Lack of support
- Poor working conditions

Remember, finding the right job is all about finding the right fit between your strengths, personalities, and the role.

■ Can you be a Team Player and Learn How to Fit In?

Although security officers are rarely seen together, they often work in teams. Take patrolling, for instance: If the area is large enough, each officer is assigned a section of the building's perimeter. Working together, they ensure the entire perimeter is secure.

A good security officer should show dedication and determination as an active team member. He/she should cooperate with everyone despite personal differences and be honest and open with his/her team members.

Joel Garfinkle (*Author of 7 books on leadership, and one of the country's most effective and innovative executive coaches*) wrote, Strong team players are the backbone of any team. When others fail, these people venture on with strong resolve and persistence, committed to getting the job done. Most people can list the qualities of bad team members without struggling too hard, but do you know what qualities great team players share?

HERE ARE FIVE QUALITIES THAT MAKE A GOOD TEAM PLAYER, GREAT:

Always reliable.
A great team player is constantly reliable, not just some of the time. You can count on them to get the job done, meet deadlines, keep their word, and provide consistent quality work. With excellent performance, organization, and follow-through on tasks, they develop positive work relationships with team members and keep the team on track.

Communicates with confidence.
Good team players might silently get the work done, but shy away from speaking up and speaking often. Great team players communicate their ideas honestly and clearly and respect the views and opinions of others. Clear, effective communication done constructively and respectfully is the key to getting heard.

> Great team players lack excessive ego or concerns about you. They are quick to point out the contributions of others and slow to seek attention for their own. They share credit, emphasize team over self, and define success collectively rather than individually. It is no great surprise, then, that humility is the single greatest and most indispensable attribute of being a team player.
>
> - *Patrick Lencioni*

Does more than asked.
While getting the work done and doing your fair share is expected of good team players, great team players know that taking risks, stepping outside their comfort zones, and coming up with creative ideas is what it'll take to get ahead. Taking on more responsibilities and extra initiative sets them apart from others on the team.

Adapts quickly and easily.
Great team players don't passively sit on the sidelines and see change happen; they adapt to changing situations and often drive positive change themselves. They don't get stressed or complain but are flexible in finding their feet in whatever is thrown their way.

Displays genuine commitment.
Good team players are happy to work 9-5 and receive their paycheck at the end of the month. Great team players take the time to make positive work relationships with other team members a priority and display a genuine passion and commitment toward their team. They come to work with the commitment of giving it 110% and expect others on the team to do the same.

You don't have to be extroverted or indulge in self-promotion to be a great team player. Great team players sport all kinds of personalities. You just need to be an active participant and do more than your job title states. Put the team's objectives above yours and take the initiative to get things done without waiting to be asked. In return, you will build positive perception, gain more visibility, and develop influential connections to get ahead in your career.

■ Are you an Effective Communicator?

Being a great communicator is one of the vital skills of a Security officer. The ability to effectively communicate with others is not only critical in the daily performance of their job, but also in our daily lives as it is very important to one's professional growth and development.

A good security officer should communicate well with co-workers, clients, and any other person he/she deal with in the course of work. They must know how to speak clearly and use correct wording to convey messages. Communication must be transmitted so that it is received and understood as intended.

Documentation
Communication doesn't only apply verbally, but also in writing. Another huge link in a security officer's responsibility is documentation and report writing. Documentations

are reflections of people's whereabouts, what happened, communications, who did what, and notifications made.

Most security officers must accurately report their shift activities each day.

Security officers are required to document all accidents/incidents on client premises accurately. These reports must be written to accurately reflect what happened. Once signed, reports become official documents that can be subpoenaed as court records if needed. Without clearly articulating what happened and using incorrect grammar and punctuation, these records become null and void.

A security officer's communication must be able to achieve the following goals: comply with rules and regulations, gain information, direct and control conduct, and foster positive customer reactions. Effective communication skills best accomplish these goals. **The ability to communicate in a friendly manner indicates the security officer's maturity level.**

If you answered "NO" to five or more of these questions........ Chances are, you are not yet ready for a security position. However, if you still want to pursue it, start taking the necessary steps to improve.

While these highlighted tasks can improve security, it's also important to understand that other key personality traits (i.e., a passive demeanor, a poor self-image, low stress tolerance, etc.) may not be as easy to overcome. If you're currently dealing with some personality-related roadblocks, you should seriously reconsider if private security is a good fit for you.

Bottom Line: Before applying for that security position, be very honest with yourself about your skill set, your personality type, and your habits. It's true that the world is full of security officers who wouldn't be able to pass the above test, but we have a name for those people: "BAD SECURITY OFFICERS." Don't become yet another member of that infamous club. Instead, if you believe you have the potential to be a security professional, set your sights on becoming the best security professional you can be. Do that by getting your personal issues in check and developing the proper skills before sending your resume to a security provider.

SUMMARY

- Just because someone else thinks you are ready for a security position doesn't mean you are.

- How you feel about yourself has the most significant impact on how you view others.

- Without confidence in yourself, it will be hard to get others to have confidence in you.

- Being a Security Officer requires the following characteristics.

  - Being able to set a good example for the team
  - keeping your personal feelings from getting in the way of performing your job
  - disciplined in doing what's needed
  - knowing how to receive constructive criticism
  - handling pressure
  - being a team player and learning how to fit in
  - being an effective communicator

- The ability to communicate in a friendly manner indicates the security officer's maturity level.

- What makes a good security officer will largely depend on their willingness to adapt and ability to develop the new skills needed for the position.

CHAPTER 2
DUTIES & RESPONSIBILITIES

Learning objectives

After reading this chapter, you should be able to

- Define why Security needs to be licensed.

- Identify the main 3 categories of Private Security Services?

- Define the Security Officers' primary responsibilities.

- Identify Security Officers' Job Requirements.

- What is a Code of Ethics

Roy Wyatt

DUTIES AND RESPONSIBILITIES

CHAPTER 2
DUTIES & RESPONSIBILITIES

What is a Security Officer? You may have heard the terminology Security Guard or Security Officer. A Security Officer (or security agent) is a person who is paid to protect property, assets, or people. They are usually privately and formally employed civilian personnel, and they may be armed.

Security officers are generally uniformed and act to protect property by maintaining a high-visibility presence to deter illegal and inappropriate actions, observing (either directly, through patrols, or by watching alarm systems or video cameras) for signs of crime, fire, terrorism, or disorder, then taking action and reporting any incidents to their client and emergency services as appropriate, according to Wikipedia.

While this definition covers a broad perspective and accounts for most jobs, it sometimes pales in comparison to what actually transpires on some client sites.

Company policies and procedures govern Security Officers. Their duties and job requirements will vary by the site they're working on. Since every client site is different, so will their responsibilities.

Define why Security is so important?

You may have heard Security Officers being called some unfortunate names, such as flashlight cops and rent-a-cops, and they are often portrayed to the public in the movies as lazy slobs, while sitting around eating and sleeping all day and exercising poor judgment. This is rather common. A quick turn on the television will justify this every time. The truth is that security is a very respectable job path. Security Professionals are the unsung heroes of many businesses and establishments, covering most career fields. They also protect our banks, museums, malls, and other important areas.

■ Licensing Requirements

Most states require security officers/guards to be licensed. Each country has its laws and governing practices for becoming a security guard, so it's essential to check the rules and legislation in your own state.

In Virginia, registration is required for security guards. The <u>Virginia Department of Criminal Justice</u> makes the regulations regarding licensing. Certain criteria must be met before a license is approved. Those requirements are:

- Be at least 18 years old
- Finger print cards
- Mentally competent
- No drug or alcohol use or dependence
- Must successfully pass a drug test
- No felony convictions
- No disabilities that would prevent performance of duty
- Submit to a criminal background check
- Successfully complete 18 hours of required training

To carry weapons, such as batons, firearms, and pepper spray, security officers must go through additional training mandated by the state. Some states require a license to carry each item while on duty. Some officers are required to complete police certification for special duties. Virginia's training standards for security are identical to police training regarding firearms (shotgun and handgun), but they do not place licensing requirements for other items carried; only the training provided must be documented. Several security companies have also become certified in RADAR and trained their sworn special police officers to use it on protected properties in conjunction with lights/sirens, allowing them to enforce traffic laws on private property legally. <u>Armed Guards/Officers must renew their registration every two (2) years. A completion of four hours of refresher training is also required.</u>

> **THINK ABOUT IT**
> Why is it important for Security Officers be licensed?

■ Types of Private Security Services

Private security has existed for a very long time, in one form or another. Although we'd like to think that we live in a world that allows for safety from personal harm, theft, or vandalism, the facts show us otherwise. Crime rates are higher than ever, and criminals are becoming much more daring and ruthless in their desperate attempts.

There is virtually a security provider specializing in any form of security. Here are the major categories of private security services you will find.

- **Personal Security**
  This service is typically used for celebrities, corporate executives, high-profile individuals, and dignitaries. Personal security is geared toward protecting a single individual. In most cases, persons of this type are most interested in hiring armed security agents (A.K.A Body Guards)

- **Executive Security**
  Executive-level security services are geared toward protecting a group of high-profile individuals. Typically, executive protection services are employed by a group of corporate or business professionals who might be traveling overseas or entering a potentially sticky situation.

- **Event Security**
  Event security is among the top-level services provided by security firms. This service involves providing extremely savvy protection agents to monitor and secure small to large events, which can range from small business parties to large political speeches.

Most firms are willing to tailor their services to meet client-specific needs. Nearly all security firms worldwide are well-versed in a vast array of situations, and most of these companies only hire off-duty (or retired) police officers and military personnel. This is because men from backgrounds such as these have been very well trained in the areas necessary to provide the absolute best security service possible.

> A significant economic justification for security personnel is that insurance companies (particularly fire insurance carriers) will give substantial rate discounts to sites that have a 24-hour presence.

As you can see, becoming a Security Officer means you will play a vital role in ensuring clients' safety and the security of people, products, or services. You will need to use your judgment, communication, and interpersonal skills, coupled with the ability to remain calm under pressure. Certain situations will also require you to think quickly on your feet while maintaining a professional manner.

Types of Security personnel
Private Security personnel are classified into two types: "Private" and "in-house." A Private Security Officer works for a private security firm and can serve a variety of clients. The *in-house* security officer is employed by the company to provide security.

Many security firms practice the "**observe, detect,** and **report**" method. Security officers are not required to make arrests, but have the authority to arrest citizens. They also act as agents of law enforcement.

■ Basic Responsibilities

Private Security Officers play many roles, and their duties and responsibilities will vary from site to site, but their primary duty is preventing and deterring crime. They are expected to patrol and inspect property to protect against fire, theft, vandalism, terrorism, and illegal activity. They will use various forms of communication and be expected to write reports outlining observations and activities during assigned shifts.

Security officers work in public and private buildings and retail and wholesale establishments.

For carrying weapons such as batons, firearms, and pepper spray, Security Officers are required to undergo additional training mandated by the state.

Security personnel are contracted and obligated to enforce company rules and act to protect lives and property. In addition to basic deterrence, Security Officers are often trained to perform specialized tasks such as arrest and control (including handcuffing and restraints), operate emergency equipment, perform first aid, CPR, take accurate notes, write detailed reports, and perform other tasks as required by contract.

While some situations will undoubtedly involve physical intervention, the majority of tasks assigned require a security guard to observe, deter, record, and report only.

■ Job Requirements

Security officers can work at airports, banks, stores, museums, and other public venues. Some even drive armored trucks. While there are no special educational qualifications, certain requirements are necessary for the job. According to Careerplanner.com, these requirements pertain to certain skills, knowledge, and abilities necessary to perform the job successfully.

1. **Excellent Character Record**
   Since security officers protect people's valuables and property, they should have an excellent character record. Officers should not use drugs and have a clean criminal record. This is also important as some security officers carry weapons.

2. **Physical Stamina**
   Physical stamina is a must for security officers. Officers often spend many hours on their feet, walking the aisles of stores, working at checkpoints, attending athletic events, and patrolling interior and exterior areas.

Anyone hired to be a security officer must have the energy and endurance to handle the job requirements.

3. **Good Writing Skills**
Security officers must be able to write effectively. A large part of their duties will require accurate reporting daily. Security officers must know how to convey what they observed in writing with a good command of the English language. Their reports, once signed, become official documents and can be subpoenaed for court records. Sometimes, an officer may be required to fill out crime reports for law enforcement officers.

4. **Good Judgment**
Security officers must use good judgment in handling situations. They may need to use force if they are threatened, and their actions can have repercussions. Security officers must make the best decision possible in every situation.

5. **Able to Concentrate**
According to careerplanner.com, security officers must be able to focus on a specific task for long periods of time without becoming distracted. This is especially true of those who work surveillance. They may spend many hours watching multiple closed-circuit television screens, trying to assess suspicious actions. Most security jobs can be relatively monotonous. Therefore, security officers must be able to stay focused on little details for long periods of time.

> A large part of their duties will require accurate reporting daily. Security officers must be able to convey what they observe in writing and have a good command of the English language.

6. **Emotional Stability**
Security officers must also be emotionally stable. In the course of providing service, they may find themselves in difficult situations and must remain level-headed and try to resolve them. Security officers can find themselves in a life-or-death situation. Any instability can distract your judgment and make matters worse.

■ Careers/Jobs

Security is such a broad spectrum and the demand continues to increase. As a result this has opened the door for careers that just over 20 years ago never existed. In today's economy, the security field has grown at an astronomical rate and their careers are virtually limited. Below are a list of careers you may find in today's security spectrum.

Accounting/finance/Insurance/Commercial, Administrative & Clerical, Ambulance Driver/PTS Front Line, Border Patrol & Protection, Business Services & Marketing, Cash Operations, Catering, Children's services, Cleaning/Portering, Corporate, Cost services/Helpdesk, Custodial, Education/Training, Engineering, Events Stewardship and Security, Firefighter/EMT/Hazmat, Guarding, Government Svcs., Healthcare, Human Resources/Health & Safety, Installation/Maintenance Repair, Investigations, IT/Software Development, Law Enforcement, Legal, Line Mgmt, Marketing/Ad writing/PR, Medical/Health/Nurses/Doctors/Forensic and Décon, National accts., Parking and Transportation Services Mgmt., Police Investigations, Prisoner Transport/Escort, Project/Program Mgmt., PTS Mgmt, Risk, Road Inspector, Sales/Retail/Business Development, Science/Energy Environment, Secretarial and Administration, Security/Protective Svcs., Security Mgmt., Strategic Mgmt., Technical Support, Telecommunications, Utility Services, and Welfare to Work.

This is a broad listing from various companies; each provider will have its own field of careers and operations.

■ Personnel

Although Security officers differ greatly from Police Officers, military personnel, and federal agents/officers, the United States has a growing proportion of security personnel with former police or military experience, including senior management personnel. On the other hand, some Security officers, particularly young people, use the job as practical experience to apply to law enforcement agencies.

Due to the complexities of the law and legal system, lawyers require extensive training. Their impact on others also dictates the need for an ethical code to govern their actions. So, let's look at the typical responsibilities and duties of a Security Officer.

> A **code of ethics** document may outline the mission and values of the business or organization, how professionals are supposed to approach problems, the ethical principles based on the organization's core values, and the standards to which the professional is held.
>
> - *Investopedia*

■ Code of Ethics

Security Officers must possess a code of ethics. They face ethical dilemmas daily and are then expected to make ethical decisions.

For companies with Security Handbooks, a code of ethics will be included. Some larger companies print information on wallet-sized cards that employees may be required to carry while on duty.

Roy Wyatt

Most decisions will come from the Security Officer's policies and procedures, but you must have the will to follow the correct path even when you would rather not and/or when policy doesn't dictate.

Your code of ethics will serve as a minimum set of behavior guidelines you are required to follow. Ethics are based on a collection of values, morals, and good judgment. An effective code reinforces ethical values so they become automatic responses. The very word "security" stands for safety, protection, comfort, and confidence. Individuals in the security profession need to live up to those words.

Here are the basic elements of every Security Officer's Code of Ethics that they should follow.

1. Always arrive at work on time and dressed appropriately.

2. Respond appropriately to the employer's needs, and treat him or her with the utmost respect.

3. Accept the responsibilities and obligations of my role as a licensed security officer. To endeavor to shield persons or property from those who would cause harm and to do so with attentive observation and reporting to law enforcement while on duty.

4. Set the example at all times;

5. Exhibit exemplary conduct;

6. To observe the precepts of truth, accuracy, and prudence, without allowing personal feelings, prejudices, animosities, or friendships to influence my judgment.

7. Maintain a safe and secure workplace;

8. Enforce all lawful rules and regulations, and do not engage in deceptive, misleading, or unlawful activities.

9. Respect and endeavor to protect the confidential and privileged information of my employer or client beyond the term of my employment.

10. Develop good rapport within the profession and strive to attain professional competence.

11. Treat others the way you would like to be treated.

12. Encourage liaison and cooperate with public and life safety officers.

13. To conduct myself with honesty and integrity and to adhere to the highest moral principles in the performance of my duties as a licensed security officer.

Large or small, even the best-managed companies can be sued. Business executives never intend to put themselves at risk, but they often are not aware of or fully understand the implications of their actions.

> **THINK ABOUT IT**
> Why is it so important for Security Officers to possess a Code of Ethics?

Delivering services is critical to the safety and security of the public; you must be every bit as accountable to the individuals you serve. Both the public and private sectors increasingly demand high-quality security technology. Equally, the security industry requires increasingly higher levels of professionalism and sophistication daily. Protection of property and persons must be combined with strict respect for laws, regulations, and a code of ethics.

SUMMARY

- A **major economic justification** for security personnel is that insurance companies (particularly fire insurance carriers) will give substantial rate discounts to sites that have a 24-hour presence. This is because having security on site increases the odds that any fire will be noticed and reported to the local fire department before a total loss occurs.

- The **licensing requirements** for Security Officers in most states consist of:

    - Be at least 18 years old
    - Finger print cards
    - Mentally competent
    - No drug or alcohol use or dependence
    - Must successfully pass a drug test
    - No felony convictions
    - No disabilities that would prevent performance of duty
    - Submit to a criminal background check
    - Successfully complete 18 hours of required training

- Three main **categories of private services** are: Personal, Executive, and Event Security.

- A **Code of Ethics** is needed because Security Professionals face ethical dilemmas daily and are expected to make ethical decisions.

- Private Security Officers play many roles, but their primary duty is preventing and deterring crime.

- All Security Officers must possess the **following requirements**:

    - Excellent Character Record
    - Physical Stamina
    - Good Writing Skills
    - Good Judgment
    - Able to Concentrate
    - Emotional Stability

Roy Wyatt

CHAPTER 3
RULES & STANDARDS OF CONDUCT /
POLICIES AND PROCEDURES

Learning objectives

After reading this chapter, you should be able to

- Identify the purpose of Employee Handbooks and why they are essential to employees.
- Define the importance of understanding yourself.
- Identify Security Officer's basic responsibilities.
- Identify the two categories of attendance.
- Identify some on–the–job rules and standards of conduct.
- Define the meaning of Fraternization and Nepotism.
- Define and identify some examples of Sexual harassment.
- Understand the company's Alcohol and Drug Free Policy.
- Identify some company time-keeping methods.
- Define the difference between workweek and workday
- Identify some company requirements for promotions and transfers.
- Name 3 forms you will likely use in the Security Industry?
- Define some healthcare benefits.
- Define FMLA

RULES & STANDARDS OF CONDUCT/ POLICIES AND PROCEDURES

CHAPTER 3
RULES & STANDARDS OF CONDUCT /
POLICIES AND PROCEDURES

An employee handbook, sometimes also known as an employee manual, staff handbook, or company policy manual, is a book given to employees by an employer.

Employee handbooks communicate their company's mission, policies and expectations. They are necessary guidelines that are in place to maintain a consistency and order to ensure the efficient operation of the organization. In short they are a set of rules to govern. It will identify the company policies and procedures as well as behaviors and conduct that will warrant disciplinary action if seen or committed.

Employee handbook is a valuable tool; not only for employees, but for employers as well. Employee handbooks provide guidance and information related to the organization's history, mission, values, policies, procedures, and benefits, but can also be used to avoid litigation and put staff members at ease by spelling out, in positive terms, the company's policies and expectations. Furthermore, as a condition of employment, many companies require security officers to sign a statement stating their responsibility to read, understand, and abide by its contents.

> An employee handbook is an excellent resource that presents all the information employees need about their work and workplace. Thus, it facilitates the smooth functioning of a workplace.

FOREWORD

This section contains generic information and does not represent any particular security company or provider. It is intended to give a broad perspective of the many policies and procedures individuals desiring a position in the security industry (or already in) may encounter. It is not a substitute for company employee handbooks, policies, and procedures manuals, government agencies or entities, or any other disclosures protected under federal, state, or local law or regulation.

INTRODUCTION

■ Why Security

Today's security concerns touch every facet of business, from minor accidents to major sabotage. Since September 11, 2001, the focus on security has been a top priority and concern for companies and private citizens, who are highly in demand.

Another major economic justification for security personnel is that insurance companies (particularly fire insurance carriers) will give substantial rate discounts to sites that have a 24-hour presence; for a high-risk or high-value venue, the discount can often exceed the money being spent on its security program. This is because having security on site increases the odds that any fire will be noticed and reported to the local fire department before a total loss occurs. Also, the presence of security personnel (particularly in combination with effective security procedures) tends to diminish "shrinkage" theft, employee misconduct, and safety rule violations, property damage, or even sabotage, according to the Bureau of Labor Statistics.

> Becoming a Private Security Officer means that you have a lot of career options open to you, from protecting high-profile professionals at a business to working for a celebrity to working for a store or bank. Just as the job outlook for private security guards is diverse, so are the educational and professional training

In recent years, due to elevated threats of terrorism, most security officers are required to have bomb-threat training and/or emergency crisis training, especially those located in soft target areas such as shopping malls, schools, and any other area where the general public congregates.

Security personnel may also perform access control at building entrances and vehicle gates, meaning they ensure that employees and visitors display proper passes or identification before entering the facility. Security officers are often called upon to respond to minor emergencies (lost persons, lockouts, dead vehicle batteries, etc.) and to assist in serious emergencies by guiding emergency responders to the scene of the incident, helping to redirect foot traffic to safe locations, and by documenting what happened on an incident report. Many officers are frequently contracted to respond as law enforcement until a situation at a client location is under control and/or public authorities arrive on the scene.

From a financial standpoint, utilizing private security takes the burden out of not only the worry of managing, but also negates the additional expenses that come with employees.

> **THINKABOUT IT**
> Why is it important to have
> Employee Handbooks?

Whatever your position, you have the important assignment of performing every task to the best of your ability. If you're not doing this, it isn't fair to your employer, its customers, your teammates, or to yourself. As long as you have the job, put your all into it.

■ At-Will Employment Relationships

Just as you can divorce employers for any reason, so can they. Your relationship with employers is an "at-will relationship. This means that your employer can terminate employment at any time, with or without notice, and provided it's not illegal.

To further their cause, employees must abide by company policies and procedures outlined in employee handbooks, their training, Post Orders, or communicated through their on-site chain-of-command. Their work assignment can also be changed or modified at the complete discretion of the Company

ON THE JOB – STANDARDS OF CONDUCT

■ First Day of Work / Making a Good Impression

You have landed the job, and now the important work is over. Now it's essential to do your best to impress your boss and teammates right from the start. First impressions count; your supervisor and colleagues will judge you based on how you look, act, and what you do from the very first day. And their opinion will most likely never change.

Making a good first impression is very important. There is no such thing as a second chance. Whether you like it or not, it only takes a few seconds for people to make an opinion, and often it sticks. When it comes to making a great first impression, getting it right the first time is incredibly vital. Whether you like it or not, you only get one shot at it.

Before reporting for work, you should have received adequate rest. You must be properly groomed with a clean, wrinkle-free uniform and polished shoes. All required items should accompany your uniform. No unserviceable items (ripped, torn, mutilated, etc.) should be worn.

When it comes to appearance, how you put yourself together matters more than being conventionally pretty, "says Brandy Mychals, author of How to Read a Client from Across the Room (McGraw-Hill, 2012). "A job can be over before you even sit down because the person has already made snap judgments."

You may not have noticed, but when you meet someone for the first time or simply pass them on the street, it's human nature to make assumptions about them: He's conceited and lazy, she's rich and friendly, that little girl is a brat. And you may have wondered what people think of you the first time they lay eyes on you.

Well, let's take a look. Here are some things people rate you by so you can make that tenth of a second count and wow everyone at first sight.

Arrive to work early

Arrive at your job site about **15 minutes early**, but not too much before then. This demonstrates passion and responsibility. Just as you planned to arrive at your interviews, do the same for your job. It may also be a good idea to take a test drive to this location, especially if you're unfamiliar with the traffic flow. Being early allows you time to collect your thoughts and think about how to confront the day.

> Define why is it important to make good first impressions?

Prior to reporting to work, you should receive your location of work assignment, including name and location of assignment, date and time to report, and check-in procedures from the recruiter/hiring personnel. Ensure you understand these instructions and are on post at the designated time. Besides that, other officers may depend on you so they can be relieved on time.

Be dressed appropriately when reporting for work

Your appearance is the first thing noticed wherever you go. Your Security officer uniform is a vital piece in the daily performance of security officer duties, which is a deterrent. Most security officers wear a uniform. This consists of a shirt, pants, a badge, possibly a tie or hat, and perhaps a jacket. The Security Officer, who arrives to work unshaven with a wrinkled uniform, unpolished shoes, and a general appearance that looks like the Officer just got out of bed, might as well find another job! This impression given to everyone is that this Officer doesn't care and is immediately written off as an ineffective member of the Security team. This person may be the most qualified in the field, but they have already impaired their potential for success. Always perform a self-inspection before going to work. Ensure you are mentally prepared, well-rested, and ready to work.

Always give the person training you the benefit of the doubt

If you have prior experience, chances are you have worked in different posts. This experience is great, and most companies will agree. However, this can also cause a sense of "cockiness or know it all".

The best career-related advice I ever received came from my former boss on my first day of work. He told me to listen and observe before suggesting any changes. I took that advice and have used it in other situations, both in and out of the workplace. While innovation is a good thing, it is important to be mindful of workplace dynamics. If you enter an environment where routines are already in place, a newcomer walking in and talking about "better ways" to do things will often be met with negative reactions. Why? First, you know nothing about why they do things the way they do. Second, you haven't gained the trust of your co-workers. Finally, people, by nature, are threatened by change.

By listening and observing, you will gain a lot. You will learn about the environment in which you are now a part. You will find out about the people you are working with. You may save yourself from making a major, public mistake -- you are the new kid on the block while your co-workers have been around longer. Learn from their collective experience.

Keep your ear to the grapevine but don't contribute to it

The *grapevine* should be considered the unofficial office newsletter. It is important to pay attention to what is being said. You can gain valuable insight into office dynamics, co-workers' personalities, and who to stay away from on a particular day.

It is more important not to contribute to the grapevine. This holds especially true when you are new. You don't want to begin your career with a reputation for being a gossiper. And remember how small a world it truly is. Your reputation can follow you for years to come.

Ask questions

When you first join a new team, people expect you to have questions - lots of them. This shows you have done your homework and have enthusiasm for learning. Take advantage of this opportunity and a fresh start. Once you have gotten your "feet wet," you will be expected to know and contribute more. Plus, by gaining insight before you dive into actually working and finding a routine, you'll set yourself up for early success.

Body language

Most people aren't aware and rarely consider their body language when dealing with others. However, body language is a crucial part of first impressions. From posture to looking at the clock every five minutes, these actions will speak very loudly.

Being aware of your body language can often result in immediate improvements. But most people aren't aware. Habits are often difficult to break, and they often involve emotions.

Here are some of the worst body language mistakes you can make.

- **Slouching**—Bad posture signals to others that you lack confidence, self-esteem, or energy.

- **Weak Handshake** - A handshake that isn't firm signals a lack of authority. One that is too firm could make you seem overly aggressive.

- **Avoiding eye contact**—Avoiding looking someone in the eyes can signal deception or a lack of respect.

- **Fidgeting and Touching Hair** – Fidgeting and playing with hair or clothes can reveal excessive energy, which signals discomfort or anxiety.

- **Folding Arms** – This stance creates a sense of being closed off and may signal to others that you are disinterested in them or don't buy into their message.

- **Glancing at the Clock**—Looking at the clock or your watch or even looking past a person you're speaking with will communicate disinterest or arrogance.

- **Frowning or Scowling** – Scowls and frowns, often unintentional and unconscious, communicate unhappiness and disagreement.

Once on duty, you should receive a Post Instructions/Procedures Manual informing you of your on-duty procedures. It is imperative to become familiar with these documents, as they describe your job duties and actions to take when faced with certain situations.

> Define some body languages to avoid on a first impression?

■ Basic Responsibilities

Performance standards provide the employee with specific performance expectations. They are the observable behaviors and actions that explain how the job is to be performed.

<u>Here are the basic responsibilities of a Security Officer.</u>

- Be mentally alert and prepared to work at all times
- Arrive at your post on time (not just getting to work) and ensure you are in
- proper uniform - Be neat, clean, and well-groomed
- Follow all instructions from your Supervisor
- Do not leave your post unless properly relieved
- Know your post orders and be familiar with any other procedures manual associated with your job requirements.
- Maintain and respect all company/client-issued property
- Understand and obey all policies and procedures
- No eating, smoking, or drinking except where authorized
- Perform your duties in a courteous and professional manner
- Maintain all equipment and logs
- Keep all licensing requirements up-to-date
- Be alert during the shift and report any and all suspicious activities
- Never allow anyone to enter the area without proper authorization
- In the event of an emergency or unusual situation, notify your Supervisor/appropriate personnel
- Report all accidents and incidents in a timely fashion

> The overall benefit of a confidentiality agreement is to protect a business's proprietary information by restricting an employee or client from sharing certain information with others.

■ Maintaining Confidential Information

Upon hiring, employees are required to sign the Company's Employment Agreement as a condition of employment. In connection with this agreement, the handling of confidential information will be outlined.

As a condition of employment, you may not disclose any proprietary information about the details of the employer's business or the employer's secret processes, plans, formulas, data, or machinery, or their clients. Any information unique and valuable to the business operations must be kept secret.

■ ID Cards and Licensing/Registration

Some accounts may require Identification (ID) cards issued to Security Officers for Identification and access control purposes. These cards are the property of the business and must be worn at all times while on duty. They enable you to identify yourself to clients, other employees, local and state authorities, and the general public.

ID cards, if lost or stolen, must be reported immediately, and a replacement issued if necessary.

State licensing regulations may also be a requirement. When working as a licensed security officer, you may be required to have in your possession your state-issued license or registration card. If found working without it, you may be subject to disciplinary actions up to and including termination. The security provider can also be fined.

■ Reporting Responsibilities

It is every security officer's responsibility to report any/all violations. Security companies and clients rely on the officers to uphold this standard.

When you observe potential violations of the law or the company's policies and procedures, it must be reported - even if you violated it, or especially if you did. Failure to do so could pose a risk to the company, themselves, or co-workers. Depending on the circumstance, it can also warrant disciplinary actions up to and including termination.

> Define why reporting is so important to the security profession.

Understand that no matter how well you do your job, the time will come when you will need to fill out an Incident Report because someone has attempted to bring harm to the person, place, or thing you have been hired to protect. Or maybe there's a medical emergency on-site. Knowing how to fill in that Incident report properly can affect how the job is done in the future and whether or not the client continues to work with the company that has hired them.

I once had a Security officer who, while patrolling, crashed the client's Golf Cart inside the warehouse. Not thinking anyone saw the accident, he completed his rounds, turned the Golf Cart in, and proceeded with business as usual. After his shift ended, he signed out and left without saying a word. The next morning, the Golf cart was found by the client's employees with very extensive damage, but had not been reported. After a quick review of the video footage, it was determined that one of my security officers was responsible. Needless to say, I terminated his employment immediately. This could have been avoided. However, he would have received disciplinary counseling, reporting it could have potentially saved his job.

As noted earlier, Security officers can also receive discipline up to and including termination if it is found that they willfully failed to report a violation.

If Security officers are uncomfortable reporting a violation to their immediate chain of command, companies usually have hotlines for this as well. This can be done anonymously, without disclosing any personal information.

■ Attendance Policy

The company depends heavily on its employees in order to meet client's commitments; therefore, dependability, attendance, punctuality and commitment to doing your job are essential. As such, officers must report to work on their scheduled work days as required and any repeated absences or tardiness's will be grounds for disciplinary up to and including termination.

There are two categories of absences

1. <u>Non-chargeable (Excused)</u>: These are absences that will not be charged against employees, such as:

    *   absences/tardiness due to injury or illness with supporting documentation
    *   Absences/tardiness approved in advance
    *   shift switches, and
    *   those protected under law or Company policy

2. <u>Chargeable (Unexcused)</u>: These are absences that will count against employees for missing time from work. Some reasons can be:

    *   calling off last minute
    *   no call-no show
    *   arriving late to work for unexcused reasons, and
    *   injury/illness without supporting documentation

> Regardless of how well you perform your job, nothing else matters if your attendance is not up to par.

Call-off procedures:
In the event of unforeseen circumstance where you cannot work your scheduled shift, you must contact your Supervisor, Operations or Account Manager at least 4 hours in advance.

A record of absenteeism and lateness is tracked, maintained and becomes part of the employees personnel file. If you are absent three (3) days or more because of injury/illness, you are required to bring written documentation before returning to work.

Failure to follow the company attendance policy will result in disciplinary action, including termination.

■ Rules and Standards of Conduct

Employee Conduct and Work Rules

There are general performance guidelines and on-the-job standards of conduct. All companies require the establishment of certain standards of behavior.

The following list is an example of violations that may result in disciplinary action up to and including termination.

1. Failure to report for work, and/or without proper notification
2. Leaving your post/job without permission
3. Failure to follow clock-in/timekeeping procedures to include falsifying time-keeping records
4. Violation of uniform and appearance standards
5. Failure to follow instructions
6. Driving a vehicle under the influence of alcohol or illegal drugs
7. Possession of illegal drugs/alcohol
8. Entering unauthorized areas without permission
9. Unauthorized possession of weapons
10. Disorderly conduct on Company, client property
11. Insubordination or refusal to follow lawful instructions of a Supervisor
12. Purposeful damage or theft of Company, client, or other persons property
13. Dating or engaged in a romantic or sexual relationship with someone on-site without disclosing it
14. Violation of policy that results in loss of funds, injury or death
15. Sexual Harassment and/or Discrimination
16. Inappropriate, abusive or offensive language
17. Violation of Post Orders
18. Sleeping or dozing while on duty
19. Unauthorized use of Client/Company property or equipment
20. Filing a false claim of work-related injury
21. Failure to perform job duties satisfactorily
22. Failure to meet company uniform and appearance standards
23. Refusal to accept overtime when necessary
24. Engaged in horseplay, pranks, on company property
25. Negligence or carelessness with company/client property
26. Sexual conduct of any type in the workplace

These are serious offenses. So much is expected that you must always remain focused of your duties and responsibilities. Clients and Security Company's expect you giving your best at all times. You, as a Security Professional are "*the face*" of the clients business. The higher your standards, the better perception customers will have of the clients business and services.

■ Uniform

The uniform is a very important part of being a security officer. It sets an officer apart from the general population as an individual in a position of authority. However, its primary purpose is to serve as a deterrent to criminal activity. When a would-be criminal sees an officer in uniform, this provides a strong deterrent to crime or criminal activities. An officer in plainclothes would not provide the same warning.

Security providers will provide you with all required uniforms, excluding socks, shoes, and belt (except where duty belts are provided to armed officers). How many sets will be determined by your employment status.

There are three (3) main types of uniforms: Hard Profile, Soft Profile, and Customer Specific. Which style will be determined by clients and will vary from location to location.

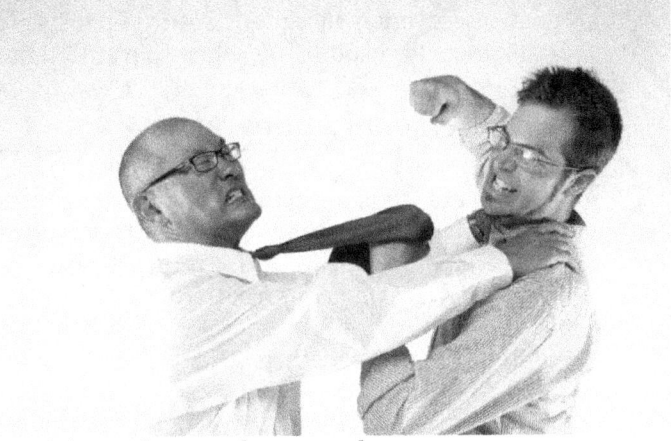

While on duty, you are required to be in complete uniform at all times. Except when travelling to/from work, uniforms are not permitted to be worn outside of work or while off duty. Violation of this policy can be grounds for disciplinary action, including termination.

Two employees engaged in a fist fight

The following are uniform requirements while on duty.

1. You must be in the company's provided uniform at all times while on duty. The only authorized civilian attire is underclothes (t-shirts/underwear, socks, and shoes).

2. You must purchase your own footwear, which will be specific to your location of work. Footwear must be black in color, closed-toe, clean, and in good working condition. If a specific type of footwear is required, the company will typically pay for the cost of the footwear or provide reimbursement.

> **THINKABOUT IT**
> Why is appearance so important?

3. If identification badges are issued, they must be worn where they are visible at all times. If lost, please notify your supervisor or appropriate personnel to get a replacement.

4. You must supply your own socks. Socks must be dark in color. Light colored socks are not permitted to be worn with the uniform.

If your uniform becomes unserviceable for any reason, notify your account manager immediately to get a replacement. If you lose or destroy the uniform, the company reserves the right to require you to pay the replacement cost, where permitted by law. In the security industry, most security providers have three uniform styles: hard look, Soft look, and Customer-specific look. The client designates which style.

In the event you leave the company, all uniforms and/or equipment must be returned. In the event you cannot return items belonging to the company, you may be held financially responsible, where permitted by law.

■ Personal Appearance

Appearance is everything to security professionals. The Impact of a Security Officer's appearance can send a powerful message to those they are assigned to protect and those who want to do harm. As a result, you are expected to display a professional appearance and conform to the company's appearance standards at all times.

Benefits of a security officer's uniform and appearance.

- Provides instant recognition
- Peace of mind for employees and customers
- Greater deterrence of crimes
- Creates a sense of pride and belonging for the officer
- Is a reflection of the professionalism of the client in addition to the security company itself

Your appearance will help determine the level of respect you command and the public's impression of the clients, customers, and company you work for.

Your appearance will help determine the level of respect you command, and the public's impression of the client, its customers and company you work for.

Security officers in clean, crisp uniforms with tucked-in shirts, pressed pants, and shined shoes convey more authority than guards wearing ill-fitted shirts and worn jeans. A professional uniform naturally demands more respect. These minimum standards below are mandatory

Here are some basic appearance standards you will find in the Industry:

- **Hair**
  - Clean, neat, and groomed
  - Length should not extend past the shirt collar, or be pulled away from the face, and secured
  - No extreme hairstyles - if dying, hair must be in a natural color

- **Facial Hair**
  - Sideburns must not extend past the earlobe / neatly trimmed
  - Mustaches must be neatly trimmed and formed to the contour of the face

- **Personal Grooming**
  - Makeup must be worn conservatively
  - Bathing and use of deodorant/antiperspirant are required
  - Perfume, cologne, and aftershave must be used in moderation
  - Fingernails clean and trimmed – no extreme colors or length.

- **Jewelry**
  - Watches and tie clips permitted – bracelets and chains are not permitted
  - Only one ring per hand permitted – must not be unreasonable large
  - One set of earrings allowed, not to exceed a dime in diameter
  - No nose, tongue, or eyebrow jewelry worn

- **Additional items**
  - Visible tattoos and body art are prohibited
  - No extreme style of eyeglasses (must be conservative) – Sunglasses are only permitted to be worn outside in sunny weather. They must not interfere with your duty.

■ No Fraternization or Nepotism

This policy prohibits anyone from being in a Supervisory position over family members or anyone with sexual or romantic involvement. The reason is that, because of an employee's familiar status or involvement with another employee, they are more likely to overlook or bypass a policy or procedure that could jeopardize the client's operation. This information must be disclosed up front, and failure to do so could have serious consequences.

If found in this situation, companies reserve the right to remove one or both employees. If this is not possible, employees may be forced to resign or be terminated.

Fraternization in the workplace encompasses relationships that go beyond the normal scope of employee interactions.

This does not prohibit employees from dating a co-worker outside of work with no supervisory overlap; it still may impact the sexual harassment and discrimination policy.

■ Disciplinary Process

Disciplinary action will be taken when Company policies, procedures, and/or work rules have been violated. When violated, it is the Supervisor's responsibility to initiate a program of disciplinary steps to address the problem.

There are four levels of action primarily used in the disciplinary process.

- verbal warning,
- written warning,
- final written and/or with suspension
- termination

Depending on the severity of the policy violation, the company reserves the right to skip any step in the progressive disciplinary process and move straight to termination if deemed necessary. For instance, using profanity may warrant a final warning or termination on the first offense.

The length of time between violations will also be taken into consideration. If twelve months have passed since the employee received a final written warning, termination may not be warranted, although it's the next level in the progressive disciplinary process. This will be at the discretion of the account manager. The company reserves the right to terminate employees "at will," with or without cause, at any time, for any reason.

■ Using Company Telephone, Internet, and Electronic Devices

As a Security professional you will likely be assigned to contracts where you will have access to telephone, radio, computer or other electronic devices. If so, understand they are only permitted to be used strictly for Company purposes.

Except where authorized, the use of company property for personal business is strictly prohibited.

The Company also reserves the right to monitor usage to enforce this policy. If found in violation, disciplinary action, including financial reimbursement, may be authorized.

GENERAL POLICIES AND PRACTICES

■ Open Door Policy

If you desire to speak with someone in management, their door is always open to discuss any ideas on how to improve company processes and procedures. The company welcomes your input and any ideas on how to achieve company objectives.

■ Concern Resolution Process

No workplace environment is completely without employee differences. Sooner or later, concerns are expected to arise. When they do, companies have formal processes to address and/or correct issues. Workplace concerns can take many forms, and if not addressed, they can detract from an employee's success and fulfillment.

When issues arise, Security Officers are encouraged to use their chain of command to get problems resolved. This process allows for each person in the complainant's command to listen to all the facts before making a judgment. In most cases, issues are resolved at the first level (site/shift Supervisor). If not, and the complainant isn't satisfied, issues then escalate to the next person in the Security Officers chain-of-command. That may be the Account Manager, DM (District Manager), or Branch Manager.

> **Chain of command** is an official hierarchy of authority that dictates who is in charge of whom and of whom permission must be asked.

Leaders have been placed into positions based on their ability, experience, training, and equipped to address and handle concerns. For this reason the chain-of-command should be followed. However, not all issues will or can be handled by on-site Supervisors or Managers. Some issues may be too sensitive, has nothing to do with the job, an informing someone on-site may cause more harm than good. Some may prefer to remain anonymous.

When discretion is needed, most companies have hotlines setup employees can use to make department officials aware of their concerns. Employees also can remain anonymous if they chose to.

■ Equal Employment Opportunity

According to eHow, workers enjoy protections under federal and state labor laws. Employers bear the responsibility for complying with these laws. The U.S. Equal Employment Opportunity Commission ensures that U.S. workers are not victims of discrimination based on protected personal characteristics. Each employer must create a policy to show its commitment to a discrimination-free workplace.

The **Equal Employment Opportunity Act** of 1972 is the act which gives the Equal Employment Opportunity Commission (EEOC) authority to sue in federal courts when it finds reasonable cause to believe that there has been employment discrimination

An employer expresses its position on equal employment opportunity in a written policy. This policy should satisfy federal requirements and be specific to your organizational culture. This policy basically states that the company cannot unlawfully discriminate on the basis of race, color, creed, national origin, physical disability, ancestry, mental disability, marital status, sex, genetic, etc. Decisions of Employment will be based on the individual's qualifications and not on any discriminatory measures.

■ Reasonable Accommodations

In compliance with state and federal laws, companies must comply with laws governing individuals with disabilities. This is an adjustment made to accommodate employees based on certain needs. These adjustments can be for religious, academic, or employment needs. They are designed to assist the employee in the performance of their duties provided it does not cause any undue hardship, or pose any threat to others or the company.

Reasonable accommodations are done on a case-by-case basis, and employees need to inform their employer if this is needed in the daily performance of their duties. Once known, companies will attempt every means necessary to accommodate the request in accordance with applicable laws.

In reviewing requests, the employer may also ask to provide any additional information to accompany request in evaluating whether to grant or deny employees request.

■ Discrimination and Harassment

Identify some examples of Sexual Harassment

Discrimination and harassment will not be tolerated in the workplace. Discrimination on the basis of color, sex, genetic characteristics or genetic information, pregnancy, age, religious creed, national origin, mental/physical disability, marital status, political activities, affiliations, or other legally protected characteristics of the person is prohibited.

According to the Department of State, companies are required to provide a workplace that is free from sexual harassment. Sexual harassment in the workplace is against the law. If it is determined that an allegation of sexual harassment is credible, it will require prompt and immediate corrective action.

What Is Sexual Harassment?
Unwelcome sexual advances, requests for sexual favors, and other verbal or physical conduct of a sexual nature constitute sexual harassment when:

1) An employment decision affecting that individual is made because the individual submitted to or rejected the unwelcome conduct; or

> A victim of sexual harassment can be a man or a woman. The victim can be the same sex as the harasser. The harasser can be a supervisor, co-worker, other Department employee, or a non-employee who has a business relationship with the Department.

2) The unwelcome conduct unreasonably interferes with an individual's work performance or creates an intimidating, hostile, or abusive work environment.

Certain behaviors, such as conditioning promotions, awards, training, or other job benefits upon acceptance of unwelcome actions of a sexual nature, are always wrong.

Harassment at workplace: Boss is seducing and flirting with secretary in office.

Unwelcome actions such as the following are inappropriate and, depending on the circumstances, may in and of themselves meet the definition of sexual harassment or contribute to a hostile work environment:

- Sexual pranks, or repeated sexual teasing, jokes, or innuendo, in person or via e-mail;
- Verbal abuse of a sexual nature;
- Touching or grabbing of a sexual nature;
- Repeatedly standing too close to or brushing up against a person;
- Repeatedly asking a person

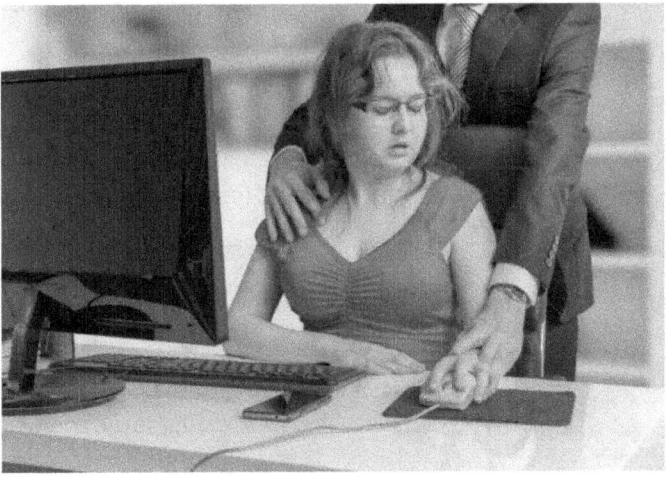

to socialize during off-duty hours
- when the person has said no or has indicated he or she is not interested (supervisors in particular should be careful not to pressure their employees to socialize);
- Giving gifts or leaving objects that are sexually suggestive;
- Repeatedly making sexually suggestive gestures;
- Displaying or showing sexually explicit material, including photographs, cartoons, or other materials, in the workplace;
- Off-duty, unwelcome conduct of a sexual nature that affects the work environment.

This list is by no way comprehensive. As a general rule of thumb, employees should not engage in any conduct or behavior that is offensive to others in the workplace.

▪ Alcohol and Drug-Free Workplace

Rest assured, there will be a policy regarding the use of drugs and alcohol in the workplace. The use of drugs hinders performance and is also a major contributor to all kinds of safety and health-related problems. Companies strive to maintain a safe and hazard-free environment for all their employees, and therefore, drugs, including any substance abuse, are strictly prohibited.

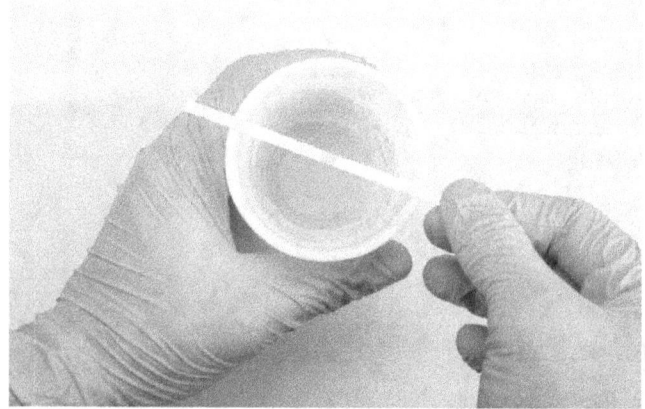

Medical Urine Test Examined By Doctor With The Help Of Urine Test Strip

To uphold this goal, the company reserves the right to test you prior to employment, randomly, annually, and/or for reasonable suspicion.

If you are required to use any prescribed medication, you must disclose this information up front. Do not wait until after employment.

Some companies will have self-referral programs to encourage officers with problems to seek help. Please consult your Company Handbook or speak with your Human Resources representative.

COMPENSATION / PAY PRACTICES

Wages
Wages are the compensation that Security officers will be paid for services. Since private security is contracted, employee wages are based on client bill rates.

Companies are in business to provide a service, but to do this, they must be compensated. All security services provided are performed at a markup rate from the security officers' wages. For instance, the Client is paying $15.00 hourly per officer for services rendered to American Securities. Based on American Securities' current markup, the security officer's pay rate will be $11.00 an hour. All markup is different, and each company will have its own. Although it's not always customary for clients to know Security officers' wages, most will. In some instances, security officer wages will be written in the contract.

■ Payment Methods

Several methods of payment may be found in the security industry to better accommodate the various needs of security officers.

Direct Deposit
This has become the preferred method of payment by a lot of companies. This may also be a requirement. With direct deposit, there's virtually no hassle. Employees only need to provide their banking information to their Security Company. On payday, employee funds will be electronically wired directly to their account of choice and ready for pick-up whenever needed. Most money is usually there by the morning hours - usually before 8 am in most cases.

Pay cards
This is also beginning to be a popular method. Pay cards are used just like bank debit or credit cards. Instead of going directly into a bank, funds are deposited onto the card, which can be used at all bank tellers and ATM locations. Just like a bank card, it will need to be activated before use. Once activated, you will need to set up a PIN number.

> In the event of a discrepancy (lost, stolen, incorrect hours, etc.), Security Companies have means of getting funds to employees in a timely manner. Chances are you won't need this. If you do, most companies have developed a process that provides an accurate and sure means of immediate retrieval.

Paper check
Some companies still offer this. Paper checks are shipped out on set days to provide time for their employees to receive them. Remember, there are a lot of variables that affect this, such as weather, putting it in the wrong box, lateness, and not getting to you at all. All of these affect your money, and quite frankly, you are taking a gamble. It's quite possible you may go years without having an issue, but the one time you do, it's usually an inconvenience.

You may find some checks are shipped to local district offices. If so, you will be required to pick yours up there. You may also have the option of having someone else pick up yours as well. If this is an option, your Security Company may need to be made aware in advance, and proof of identification is usually required.

Please check the payment options your Security Company provides and choose which is best for you.

■ Timekeeping Methods

As technology has evolved, so have security companies' timekeeping methods. Regardless of where security officers are working, security companies have developed the means of accurately inputting this data and retrieving at a moment's notice. Here are some methods you may find in the industry.

Time-sheets

This method is probably the most accurate and widely used by all security companies. Each time officers report to work, they are required to sign in/out on company time sheets. The designated individual (Supervisor, Account Manager, etc.) enters information into the company's timekeeping system, and officers are paid accordingly.

Time Sheets can be kept on or off-site, depending on the company's protocol. If not used as the main timekeeping method, they may/may not be kept as backup.

Whoever manages the account will normally input these times. If posts are remote, Time Sheets may be picked up or sent to a designated location.

Electronic Time Card System

Some accounts may have wall-mounted electronic time clocks and digital time clocks that let people clock in using a website. Whenever officers report for work, they are required to punch in/out utilizing Time Cards. Their data is automatically uploaded into the systems, and they usually manually stamp the date/time onto their sheet. The Time Cards are then collected and inputted into the system by their Manager or representative.

In most cases, the security company controls the electronic time-keeping system. However, clients may authorize security personnel to use theirs.

Client's Timekeeping System

You may encounter sites where officers are required to punch in and out using the client's timekeeping system. If so, every officer assigned to the client's site will have an identification code. When signing in, that officer's code must be entered into the system, and their time will be electronically recorded. This will oftentimes be used to compare the hours billed by the Security Company. If there is a discrepancy, the client's timekeeping method will most likely be used.

If you encounter this, be sure to clock in first using the client's timekeeping system before clocking in with your security company's timekeeping method.

Calling in

Some companies have accounts set up for Call Centers that require security officers to call in upon arriving and departing from their assigned posts. These calls are placed directly into a Call Center that keeps track of this information. From there, information is directly input into the company's timekeeping system. For identification, each officer will have a unique employee identification number.

If no officer calls in for a scheduled post, calls are routed to the appropriate personnel until the shift is covered or until it is explained why no coverage is required. If no coverage is needed, the shift will be removed

Call Center Operators will have the numbers to the accounts as well as a call tree with the accounts' chain of command. These are usually smaller contracts. Some may be a distance from the main office and/or one of a number of accounts being managed by one or multiple managers. You can see why timesheets may not be feasible since this would require a single manager to input all the timekeeping for several accounts. If so, this method would potentially open the door for possible mistakes.

> Call Center Operators will have the numbers to the accounts and a call tree with the accounts' chain of command.

I'm sure there are other methods out there, but these make up a large percentage of the industry standard. Whichever system is used, you can feel comfortable knowing it has been proven, and information will be accurately reported.

■ Overtime Pay Policies

An employer who requires or permits an employee to work overtime is generally required to pay the employee premium pay for such overtime work. For non-exempt employees, the Fair Labor Standards Act (FLSA) requires overtime pay to be at least one and one-half times an employee's regular rate of pay after 40 hours of work in a workweek.

From time to time, Security Officers may be required to work overtime. It could be as a result of a call-off, someone being sick, or running late. If doing so increases your weekly total above 40 hours, the company is legally required to pay you at the overtime rate. Exempt employees (salaried) are not entitled to receive overtime pay.

Overtime hours are only calculated from actual hours worked. That means you cannot receive overtime pay for similar days "not worked," such as vacation, sick pay, holidays, etc. You must physically work to receive overtime pay.

Additional Rules for Specific Locations
In addition to federal laws, certain non-exempt employees in states such as Alaska, Nevada, Kentucky, and Colorado have different laws governing overtime. If you live in any of these states, be certain to check the handbook.

■ Workweek / Workday Defined

Receiving pay on Friday doesn't mean the pay period ended the night before. It probably ended a week beforehand. Companies need ample time to process payments and take out the required allotments, taxes, etc. before sending out paychecks.

From a company standpoint, a workweek is defined by a continuous 168-hour period (7 days/24hours). This is important for two reasons: pay period and overtime. This time is used to define the beginning and end of each pay period. Many companies workweek begins Friday at 12:00 am and ends at the same time the following week. However, it can also be Monday through Sunday. Any questions regarding this should be directed toward your Manager of Accounts.

■ Employment Classifications

Upon being hired, every employee will fall under one of the following employment classifications.

- Fulltime
  Employees are hired to work a regular schedule of full-time hours weekly. The number of hours will depend on the security provider.

- Part-time Employees
  Employees hired to work a regular schedule with less than full-time hours.

- Temporary
  Employees are hired for a specific period of time or for the completion of a project or assignment.

- Exempt or Non-exempt
  Every employee hired will be classified as exempt or non-exempt. This means employees are eligible – or not- to receive overtime pay in accordance with local, state, and federal laws. Hourly employees (usually Security Officers) are generally non-exempt. They are paid on an hourly basis for all hours worked and are eligible to receive overtime in accordance with overtime policies. Salaried employees are not. They are exempt from receiving overtime pay.

Note: Full-time hours are normally 40-hours, but can vary depending on the Security Company. Some company's requirement may be 35 hours or less. Check your Employee Handbook.

■ Work Schedules/Shifts

Security is a client driven business that requires an officer to be on post at designated timeframes. For this reason, security providers hire officers for designated shifts to work a set, floating, or rotating schedule. Every employee schedule will be made aware of prior to hiring and beginning work.
Here's one example of a 2-set schedule.

	Sample schedule:	
Monday thru Friday	0600hrs – 1400hrs	(40hr shift)
Sat & Sun	1200hrs – 2400hrs	(24hr shift)

The 24hr clock (sometimes called military time) is usually the preferred method of timekeeping for most security providers because of the large number of problems that could be caused by confusion about time.

Whenever vacancies become available, Security Companies may hire or move officers around to accommodate open shifts/schedules. Nevertheless, all posts must be covered.

■ Site Changes/ Transfers/Promotions

The company encourages its employees to take interest in career opportunities and seek advancement. You may require more compensation, better opportunities, closer to home, and better benefits. The list goes on and on.

Employees who are already with the company and who have consistently performed satisfactorily or better are the strongest candidates for promotion. The company will always attempt to accommodate them, provided they meet the following requirements.

1. Must have no less than satisfactory performance or above, to include no disciplinary actions (including Performance Improvement Programs (PIP) within the last six (6) months.

2. The employee must have met the minimum required time on contract and/or with the company - this could range from 3 to 6 months or longer, and

3. Their current position may need to be filled. Oftentimes, this can be done within a couple of weeks,, but it will vary

Applying for a new position does not guarantee promotion. The company reserves the right to look outside the company for the best-fit employee for the position sought.

■ Performance Evaluations

Every employee deserves to know the status of their performance, from how well they are performing to areas that need improvement. It is important to periodically assess and adapt your activities to ensure they are as effective as possible.

Security officers are required to receive a performance evaluation annually from their direct Supervisor or Manager. An initial evaluation and a 30-, 60-, or 90-day evaluation may also take place.

> During performance evaluations, Officers must realize that how Supervisors and Managers see them may be different from their perception.

Evaluation helps employees identify areas for improvement and ultimately helps them realize their goals more efficiently.

An earnest evaluation takes time and should not be taken for granted. Officers deserve an earnest evaluation of their performance. Supervisors should schedule time for uninterrupted evaluations and discuss officer performance in detail. Any areas of concern or disagreement should be discussed at that time.

During an evaluation, Officers must realize that how Supervisors/Managers see them may often be different from their perception. Not understanding this can sometimes put officers in a negative mood that can be avoided.

If there are areas of concern, be sure to have the person performing the evaluation give you tips on improving these areas before the next evaluation.

After completion, each evaluation must be placed in the employee's file and a copy given to them.

■ Making Errors

We all make mistakes on forms sooner or later, but when you do, please ensure to correct them before submitting. Reports are controlled documents, and the accuracy of information is critical. Mistakes on reports can mislead, misrepresent, or void a document altogether.

Once signed, reports become official documents, and mistakes can become costly.

Security officers should proofread all documents, and if an error is noted, correct it. Since documents are only written in ink, this becomes a problem since erasing is virtually impossible. Because of this difficulty, whiteout, taping, and re-doing the document is usually the only options. If your company allows the use of these, please use them. Some clients may have a policy on the usage of these items as well when turning in documents.

Here are some things that may warrant a document to be rewritten:

- Illegibility
- Mutilation
- Crossed out words (too many)
- Misspellings
- Incorrect grammar

Be sure to know your company policy as it relates to correcting mistakes. Some companies do not allow white-out usage, while others have limits on the number of mistakes made before the entire document must be rewritten. In most cases, your supervisor should be able to inform you of the policy.

As a Security Officer, it is your responsibility to ensure your information is mistake-free.

■ Forms and Records

A large part of a security officer's job will be documentation and reporting. Not only will documents need to be created and maintained, but a record of officer activities must also be kept. The law also requires that the company keep books, records, and accounts that accurately reflect all transactions.

Records are vital to organizations and are kept for years at a time. Some must be kept permanently; others for 7 to 10 years, while a majority are kept between 1 and 3 years. Some are maintained on-site for a while and later shipped to a District Office or a more permanent storage location. Records serve as proof of transactions, procedures, incidents, personnel, whereabouts, conversations, etc., that can later be audited or subpoenaed, so legibility is of utmost importance.

> Records serve as proof of transactions, procedures, incidents, personnel, whereabouts, conversations, etc., that can later be audited or subpoenaed.

Many companies utilize systems software in conjunction with handwritten reports—both must be maintained. If reports are handwritten, please verify their legibility. Nothing is worse than seeing poorly written records that only the person who wrote them can read. For this reason, most security records are written in print instead of cursive.

"Black ink" is also the preferred method of security, as penciled information can easily be manipulated.

Be advised; if your handwriting needs improvement, it will serve you better to take classes and/or practice to bring this up to a more acceptable level. All security officer reports are subject to being seen and checked by your leaders. Clients will also have the authority to review these documents, as your actions are performed on their property. Before hiring, some managers may even require officers to take a handwriting test. I certainly did at times. Grammar and punctuation are also very important.

Daily Action Report, Daily Journal, Log Sheet

This is a daily record of the security officer's activities during his/her shift. Each day, your activities must be recorded. At the end of your shift, if you are being relieved by another officer, they must look over and sign this report. Since both of you are performing the same job, your actions will inform them of events that have transpired while indicating any expected issues or concerns. You should also verbally inform your relieving officer of any pertinent information they may need to know – this is usually called *pass downs* in the security industry. You are passing down pertinent and warranted information to the next officer coming on duty.

After completion, logs must be signed, turned in, or placed in an area designated by your Supervisor or Post Orders.

Accident / Incident Report Form

Incident Reports document situations or events that normally don't transpire from day-to-day activities, such as a medical emergency, vehicle accident, property damage, employee dispute, or bomb threat. This is a big part of an officer's responsibility and goes a long way toward validating their presence.

If you are unsure of whether a situation warrants writing an Incident Report, write it anyhow. It's always better to have one and not need it than to need one and not have it.

Only factual evidence should be documented when filling out Incident Reports, and not suspected or perceived information. You only report what was seen or heard by yourself and/or witnesses - no other information.

Security Supervisor reviewing Incident Report with employee

Incident Reports should answer the following questions: who, what, when, where, why, and how. They should be written so that third-party personnel can get a clear picture of what transpired without trying to recreate the scene.

Incident Reports require your immediate Supervisor (if on-site) to look over, verify, and sign. Additional notifications may also be required.

Incident Reporting procedures must be clearly outlined in Security Post Orders or Emergency Procedures Manual. Clients will certainly read these. Ensure they are legible, complete, and accurately reflect what happened.

All reports should be proofread, and any grammar and punctuation corrected before submitting.

Visitor/Contractor Log

These are access control logs that identify personnel entering and departing the facility. They are usually kept at entranceways to facilities where high visibility is maintained. Some contractors and visitors may have badges that will allow access; these may/may not need to sign in. Be sure to check the policy.

Everyone who does not have building access will be entered onto these logs. Some information may include: name, person visiting, nature of visit, and the company they work for. In most cases, they will be issued badges as well. Once their contact has been notified and approval given, they will be granted access, and their contact will usually come and escort the visitor. Prior to departing, the contractor/visitor will need to sign out and return any equipment issued. These forms are utilized by a majority of all security companies, but names and styles will vary. The next few pages are examples. They are generic and do not represent any particular company.

Roy Wyatt

Example: Daily Activity Report

DAILY ACTIVITY REPORT

DATE: _____

Location:		Equipment:		
Officer Name:		SHIFT:		

Description of Action:	Action Taken	Start	End

Officer on Duty Signature: _____

Relieving Officer Signature: _____

Example: Accident / Incident Report Form

ACCIDENT/INCIDENT REPORT FORM

Type of Incident: _____

Date of incident: _____ Time: _____ AM/PM

Name of injured person:_____

Address: _____

Phone Number(s): _____

Date of birth: _____ Male _____ Female _____

Who was injured person? (circle one) employee contractor

Type of injury: _____

Details of incident: _____

_____

Injury requires physician/hospital visit? Yes ___ No _____

Name of physician/hospital: _____

Address: _____

Physician/hospital phone number: _____

Signature of injured party :_____

Date: _____

Was Medical attention desired and/or required. ☐Yes ☐No

Signature of injured party _____

Date: _____

Return this form to Safety Coordinator within 24 hours of Incident.

Example: Visitors / Contractors Log

Visitor and Contractor Sign-in/Out Form

Date _____

Name		Company	Person Visited	Tel #:	Time In	Time Out
Name		Company	Person Visited	Tel #:	Time In	Time Out
Name		Company	Person Visited	Tel #:	Time In	Time Out
Name		Company	Person Visited	Tel #:	Time In	Time Out
Name		Company	Person Visited	Tel #:	Time In	Time Out
Name		Company	Person Visited	Tel #:	Time In	Time Out
Name		Company	Person Visited	Tel #:	Time In	Time Out
Name		Company	Person Visited	Tel #:	Time In	Time Out
Name		Company	Person Visited	Tel #:	Time In	Time Out
Name		Company	Person Visited	Tel #:	Time In	Time Out
Name		Company	Person Visited	Tel #:	Time In	Time Out
Name		Company	Person Visited	Tel #:	Time In	Time Out
Name		Company	Person Visited	Tel #:	Time In	Time Out
Name		Company	Person Visited	Tel #:	Time In	Time Out
Name		Company	Person Visited	Tel #:	Time In	Time Out
Name		Company	Person Visited	Tel #:	Time In	Time Out
Name		Company	Person Visited	Tel #:	Time In	Time Out

LEAVE OF ABSENCE / TIME-OFF BENEFITS

■ Vacation Time

There are several vacation plans, and each company will have its own. Typically, any paid vacation eligibility period is one year, typically. However, you may run into some that is immediate or within several months. Once you have satisfied the eligibility period, a set amount of vacation hours will be available for use. As your tenure increases, so will your vacation hours.

Example Vacation Plan

1 year on the job ---------------------------	40 hours of vacation
3 years on the job ---------------------------	80 hours of vacation
5 years on the job ---------------------------	120 hours of vacation

When applying for vacation, companies require you to give an advance notice – usually a 2-3 week notice. This allows them time to prepare and plan in advance for your expected absence. Since these are requests, you will be notified in advance whether it has been approved or not.

Anniversary bonuses
Some companies will automatically pay out any earned time-off hours instead of vacation without the officer's request. This is typically done when each employee reaches one year (Anniversary date) and every year following employment. If this is the case, it will eliminate any paid time-off. Please check your Company's policy regarding which plan they currently support.

> Define probationary period?

■ Personal and Sick Time

The accumulation of personal and sick days varies from company to company. Although companies recognize employees need time off to address personal needs, this benefit is usually reserved for regular full-time exempt and support non-exempt employees.

If employees cannot work (due to sickness or needing to care for a family member), they must notify their Supervisor reasonably early in advance. You may also be required to substantiate your absence, such as with a doctor's note from a healthcare provider. Such time will be granted without pay to employees where available.

For companies granting employees personal and sick days, the number of eligible days/hours awarded per calendar year will be in the Company handbook. The benefit must be used for its intended purposes (medical needs such as illness, injury, or doctor/dentist appointments). Employees are expected to schedule planned absences where time off minimizes disruption of workflow.

■ Family and Medical Leave (FMLA)

In accordance with the Family and Medical Leave Act (FMLA), companies with full-time employees must grant up to 12 weeks of leave for eligible employees. Within this time period, upon employees' return, they must be reinstated into their original position. *FMLA leave is unpaid*, but employees may elect to substitute their vacation pay to offset some or all of the leave if necessary.

To be eligible, the following criteria must be met:

- Employed with the company for 12 months or longer;
- Be assigned to a work site where the Company employs 50 or more employees within a 75-mile radius of that worksite, or be employed in such location in at least 20 weeks of the current year; and
- Have worked at least 1250 hours for the Company during the 12-month period immediately preceding the commencement of the leave.

Reasons for Leave:

- The birth of a child and caring for that child;
- The adoption or foster care placement of a child and caring for that child;
- To care for a spouse, dependent child, or parent with a serious medical condition; or
- The serious medical condition of the employee.

> Employees with the company 12 months or longer are eligible up to 12 weeks of FMLA leave.

While employees are on leave, the Company will continue their health benefits, including life and disability, at the same level and under the same conditions as if they continued to work. The employer and employee will continue to pay appropriate premiums.

Requesting FMLA Leave:
Ordinarily, the employee must provide 30 days' notice when the leave is foreseeable. In the event that 30 days' notice in advance is not possible, the notice must be given as soon as possible, within one or two business days of when the employee learns of the need for leave. Notices should be given to your on-duty Supervisor, Manager of Account, District/Branch, or Human Resources Department, preferably in writing.

Once received, you should receive the appropriate Leave paperwork. If you have not received paperwork within two weeks of the request, contact the District Office or your Human Resources Department.

Any request for FMLA requires medical certification made by a health care provider of the eligible employee or of the child, spouse or parent of the eligible employee as applicable. Certifications must be provided to the Company within 15 calendar days and must be an original.

Returning from FMLA Leave:
Upon returning from leave, an employee shall provide a certification from the health care provider that the employee is able to return to work when the reason for the leave was the employee's own serious medical condition. An employee returning timely from FMLA leave is generally entitled to be placed in the same or similar position to that held when the leave began. Except in special circumstances, employees who fail to return from FMLA leave in a timely manner must repay any health coverage premiums that were paid by the Company during leave.

If employees are not eligible for FMLA, they may still be granted a 30-day Medical leave, but at the sole discretion of the Company. Check the company policy.

■ Holidays

Paid Holidays will vary depending on the Security Company. Since they are likely to be different, do not assume which ones are paid. Your Employee Handbook should provide a complete list.

> Some of the most recognized holidays are:
> **Labor Day, Memorial Day, Independence Day, Thanksgiving, Christmas and New Year's Day.**

If working on these days, employees will likely be paid at the Holiday rate. This rate is usually one and a half times the employee's normal pay rate. If the employee is currently being paid twelve dollars hourly, their Holiday rate will be eighteen dollars hourly.

When a person is called for **jury duty** in the United States, that service is mandatory and the person summoned for jury duty must attend. Failing to report for jury duty is illegal and usually results in an individual simply being placed back into the selection pool in addition to potential criminal prosecution.

■ Jury Duty

As the state wants citizens to attend jury duty without fear of losing their jobs, employers must give employees time off to attend. Specific laws apply to both employers and employees when doing this, and employers do have some rights in the matter, according to eHow.

Employers should be informed as soon as employees receive notice of summons from their county or state. Ensure your employer has ample time to make adjustments due to your absence, so it does not affect the business.

Proof may also be required of the employee attending jury duty. This should not be a problem, as the court supplies jurors with documents indicating the dates and times the court was in session.

Regarding pay, although employers are not required to pay for the actual time employees served on the jury, some states do require employers to pay a portion of the time they served. State law is usually the authority unless the employee handbook or company's worker compensation states otherwise.

Some security companies will pay the officers regular wages if they must attend jury duty on a scheduled work day. Don't miss out! Please check the company policy.

■ Voting and Elections

While companies encourage you to exercise your voting privileges, you will not receive time off to do so. Since most polling locations are open extended hours, you are encouraged to vote before or after your shift, provided you cannot attend on days off. If for any reason you cannot, please consult with your Supervisor or Manager of Account. Any time off taken for this will not be paid.

■ Military Leave

For employees who serve in the Military, you will be allowed the necessary time off to fulfill this commitment. A copy of your orders will need to be submitted to your Manager. If you have accumulated vacation time, this can also be used for compensation while on leave.

Please inform your Manager as soon as you know of deployment to allow time for scheduling around your absence.

■ Bereavement Leave

Companies are not required by law to allow time off for funerals. This will need to be approved by your Manager. However, companies understand these difficult times. Employees may need time to grieve the loss of a close family member, prepare for and attend a funeral, and/or attend to any other immediate post-death matters. However, employers at their discretion may maintain bereavement policies where they are obligated to withhold.

There may be stipulations involved. Some will allow up to a certain amount of days, and deceased must be an immediate family member such as: child, spouse, parent, grandparent, etc. Any accumulated vacation may also be used if needed.

HEALTHCARE BENEFITS

Whenever employees choose companies, it's important to consider which benefits and perks matter most. Most companies now provide benefits to employees: Healthcare insurance (e.g., medical, dental), Vacation/Paid time off, and Retirement (401K) plans.

Probationary and Enrollment period
To become eligible, companies generally have a probationary period before enrollment. New employees are required to be employed with the company for a set time. This can range from 30 – 120 days. Once this period has been satisfied, employees become eligible and may enroll to take advantage of all the company offers.

> Are employers required by law to allow employees time off to attend jury duty?

With some benefits (usually health insurance), if employees choose not to participate at the time of initial eligibility, they will be required to wait until the next open enrollment period.

■ Healthcare (Medical, Dental and Vision Coverage)

On average, most companies have a probationary period between 1 and 3 months. Once this time has been satisfied, you will receive the enrollment documents in the mail. They must be completed and returned.

As soon as your benefits has been setup and processed, your card(s) will be mailed directly to you from the healthcare provider. Please look over them and ensure all the information is correct. If you have enrolled dependents, their cards will be enclosed as well. If you do not receive them, please contact your security provider at once.

If you did not enroll upon eligibility, you will usually need to wait until the next annual enrollment period, which can be a few months up to a year.

■ Retirement Plan (401K)

Most Security Providers now have 401K plans for employees. These are vested funds that, depending on the market, usually will accumulate over time. To encourage participation and growth, your Company will also contribute up to a certain percentage. They are set up for retirement use. If you continually invest over a period of time, it may provide a blanket of security long past your working years.

> Under federal law, employees are entitled to a safe workplace. Your employer must provide a workplace free of known health and safety hazards.

Since these accounts are set up for retirement (long-term use), if withdrawn beforehand, you will be penalized. I would encourage you to only withdraw if you have a dire need. Once withdrawn, it must be paid back before another loan can be granted. Your plan may also allow emergency withdrawals. Always check your plan prospectus or contact the provider directly.

Personally, I would strongly encourage everyone to participate. These funds are deducted before taxes, and depending on the amount invested, they probably won't put a major dent in your net income.

■ Reporting Workplace Injuries

Employees are directed to report all workplace injuries, regardless of severity, to their immediate supervisor before the end of their shift and file an Employee's Claim for Workers' Compensation Benefits form within 24 hours. If no supervisor is available, contact your manager as soon as possible. If no one is available, a security voice hotline will be set up where all injuries can be

SUMMARY

- **Employee handbooks** communicate their company's mission, policies, and expectations. They are necessary guidelines that maintain consistency and order and ensure the efficient operation of the organization.

- Some of a **Security Officer's basic responsibilities** include but not limited to: Being mentally alert, arriving to work on time, proper uniform, following instructions, understanding and obeying all policies and procedures, maintaining equipment and logs, keeping license up to date, not leaving your post without being properly relieved, reporting all suspicious activities and performing your duties in a courteous and professional manner.

- **Attendance** falls into two categories: Chargeable (unexcused) and Non-chargeable (excused)

- **Fraternization in the workplace** encompasses relationships that go beyond the normal scope of employee interactions.

- **Sexual harassment** is unwelcome sexual advances, requests for sexual favors, and other verbal or physical conduct of a sexual nature. Some examples include:

  - Sexual pranks, repeated sexual teasing, jokes, in person or e-mail
  - Verbal abuse of a sexual nature
  - Touching or grabbing
  - Repeatedly standing too close or brushing up against a person
  - Giving gifts or leaving objects of a sexually suggestive nature
  - Displaying sexual explicit material (photographs, cartoons, or other material)
  - Unwelcome conduct off-duty of a sexual nature that affects the work environment

- Some **timekeeping methods** on some client sites may include:
  - Time-sheets
  - Electronic Time cards
  - Client's time-keeping systems
  - Calling into call centers

- **The workweek** is defined by a 168-hour period. Workdays are 24 hours.

- Three main **forms Security Officers will** use are: Daily Journal/Action Report, Accident or Incident Report Form and Visitor and Contractor Log.

- Some **benefits** may include:
  - Vacation Time
  - Personal and Sick Time
  - Family and Medical Leave Act (FMLA)
  - Healthcare (Medical, Dental, and Vision Coverage)
  - Retirement (401K)

- **The FMLA is** a federal mandate that requires companies to grant full-time employees up to 12 weeks of leave for eligible employees.

- When a person is called for **Jury Duty** in the United States, that service is mandatory, and the person summoned must attend.

CHAPTER 4
SECURITY OFFICER TRAINING

Whether or not your state requires you to take a security guard training course before you apply for a position, you will eventually be trained in basic security guard knowledge and procedures.

The following will outline a curriculum or syllabus for a basic security guard training course:

Roy Wyatt

SECURITY OFFICER TRAINING

CHAPTER 4
SECURITY OFFICER TRAINING

Employment of Security Officers is projected to grow faster than all professions, increasing 17% through 2025. Raised safety and security concerns regarding crime, terrorism, and vandalism will continually drive this job growth.

As a result, you are entering a highly demanded field, so your chances of getting a job and becoming a Security Officer are excellent!

To be qualified, Security Officers must undergo training to ensure they are adequately prepared for the challenges these positions face on a day-to-day basis. Full-time Officers always need training and renewal for state regulations.

Security Officer training requirements vary from state to state. If you're looking to enter the industry, please refer to your state's Security Officer/Guard training requirements so you can quickly get started.

Training often includes public relations, protection, first aid, crisis deterrence, report writing, and specialized training according to specific tasks. Armed security Officers receive more rigorous training on laws and weapon retention.

Most states require these Security Officers to be licensed. Requirements vary by state, but typically include passing a background check, classroom training, and passing an examination. Continuing education is increasingly becoming a requirement for licensure renewal.

The next few pages will give you an idea of the various training most Security Officers will receive to perform their duties. Some of it will be a prerequisite to being hired (Security Officer Training Course), which will be done by the security company. Additional training may be needed based on your designated post.

These courses are designed to assist and prepare Security Officers with the necessary tools to carry out their various roles and responsibilities. They will come in handy.

As you look through the next few pages, you will quickly notice the diversity of training needed. Although many security companies may not offer these, it will be best to seek out organizations that provide additional training options, especially if you desire professional status.

Liability / Legal Aspects

This training covers the liability aspect of a security officer's job. Decisions officers make on the job may expose them and the company to liability concerns.

- Personal / Contractor / Employer
- Criminal, Civil, Administrative
- BSIS Code & Regulations
- Role of a Security Guard: Liabilities

Public Relations (Community & Customer)

This is an important skill set in the security industry. Officers need to possess a strong desire to provide excellent customer service skills. Most security officers are constantly interacting with the public, including clients, so it makes sense that they are well-trained and versed in public relations. It is also important that everyone they interact with is treated with respect and concern. Public relations can be learned, but one must be educated to learning it. It's an art, and ultimately, much like anything else, it's best to start training sooner rather than later.

- Recognizing Gender & Racial Harassment & Discrimination
- Respect: stereotyping, Attitude
- Verbal Skills / Crisis Intervention
- Introduction to Diversity
- Substance Abuse & Mental Illness
- Ethics and Professionalism (appearance, command presence, proper conduct)

Ethics & Professionalism

Security officers are constantly faced with moral decisions that affect not only themselves, but the company they work for. Clients put a great deal of trust in their security department, and it is imperative that they conduct themselves in a responsible and professional manner.

- Appearance
- Command Presence
- Proper Conduct

Observation & Documentation

This course provides officers with an understanding of the correlation between keen observation and effective documentation. Every security Officer's primary duties are to observe and report; hence, this course provides the necessary tools for every Security Officer to perform their duties at the highest standards.

- Report Writing
- Observation and Patrol Techniques
- Asking Appropriate Questions
- Observing Suspects / Suspicious Activity

Arrest Authority

If the prospect of advancing your unarmed career to being armed, this is the course you must have. The successful completion of this course, followed by a written examination, will advance your training to the next level. Officers will be taught the applicable laws relating to the use of reasonable force, including specific examples of what is considered reasonable and what is considered unreasonable.

- Overview of the Power to Arrest Manual and subject matter.
- Definition of arrest and discussion on the implications to the subject, the guard, and the company.
- Lecture/discussion on escalation and de-escalation techniques in the use of force.
- Lecture/discussion on the use of restraint techniques and their implications.
- Discussion of trespass laws and implications of enforcement.

Weapons of Mass Destruction (WMD) & Terrorism Awareness

Security officers must be alert to terrorist attacks. If an attack occurs at a facility, security officers are likely to be the first on the scene. They themselves can become victims of the attack.

This training provides officers with a basic introduction to Weapons of Mass Destruction (chemical, biological, nuclear/radiological weapons, and explosives) that is given to police officers, federal agents, and other first responders.

The various types of weapons are described and their effects explained in great detail. Officers will also be provided with the specific responses.

- The Role of a Security Officer
- The Nature of Terrorism
- Weapons of Mass Destruction
- Coordinating and Sharing of Critical Information

Communication and its Significance

This course is designed to teach security officers how vital communication is to keep an organization running smoothly and effectively. Both internal (methods of communication, protocols pursuant to contact, and other technology) and external (city/government services, police/ emergency personnel, etc.) are covered. This course will also cover

- who, when, and how to contact the necessary people;
- Radio and monitors procedures, and additional technology you may encounter
- Internal & external customers

Post Orders & Assignments

Post-order is a customized procedure based on the client's expectations that covers the security operations performed on their contract. It will outline what the security officer is responsible for, reports that need to be written, and emergency contacts. Well-put-together post-orders can make the difference between good and bad decisions in emergencies. It will also make a difference if security officers and supervisors know the expectations up front.

Good post orders that are well maintained will show clients that a security company is effectively communicating and working to the client's expected level of commitment. Overall, these will improve security officers' satisfaction because they will know exactly what is expected of them and what they need to do.

- Site Specific Training
- Equipment
- Emergency Response Issues

Employer Policies / Orientation

Prior to being welcomed as members of the security company, new hires must successfully complete a Basic Security Officer Training course. This course covers the basic skills required by security officers to succeed in their role and orients them to the new company policies and procedures, among numerous other areas.

- Employer Reports / Paperwork

- Reporting Processes / Procedures
- Tax Forms, Health Forms, Etc.
- Uniforms
- Work Schedules
- Other Internal Policies, Processes, or Procedures
- Employer Use of Force Policy

Evacuation Procedures

- Emergency Procedures Related to Life / Safety and Acts of Nature
- Working Knowledge of Evacuation Routes
- Power Outage
- Specific Points of Contact

Officer Safety

Security officers must always be observant of all types of dangerous acts and conditions. However, in their effort to be vigilant, officers can themselves become victims. Proper security safety education can help reduce the risk a security officer faces on a daily basis in the field or workplace environment. This course will equip the security officer with the knowledge needed to make split-second decisions and ensure the safety of themselves and those around them.

- Threat Assessment
- Subject Contact
- Safety Awareness
- Bloodborne Pathogens
- Environmental / Hazardous Materials

Fire Prevention and Response

Arrests, Search & Seizure - This teaches security officers to understand their authority and limits as it relates to the following.
- US Constitution & Amendments Impacting Guard Responsibilities
- Loss Prevention
- Use of Force

Access Control

Bomb Threat

Dealing with Trespassers
- Open Land
  - Private Property / Building

- Public Property
- Places of Public Accommodation/Public Access

Laws, Codes, Regulations and Ordinances

- Specific to Post Assignment

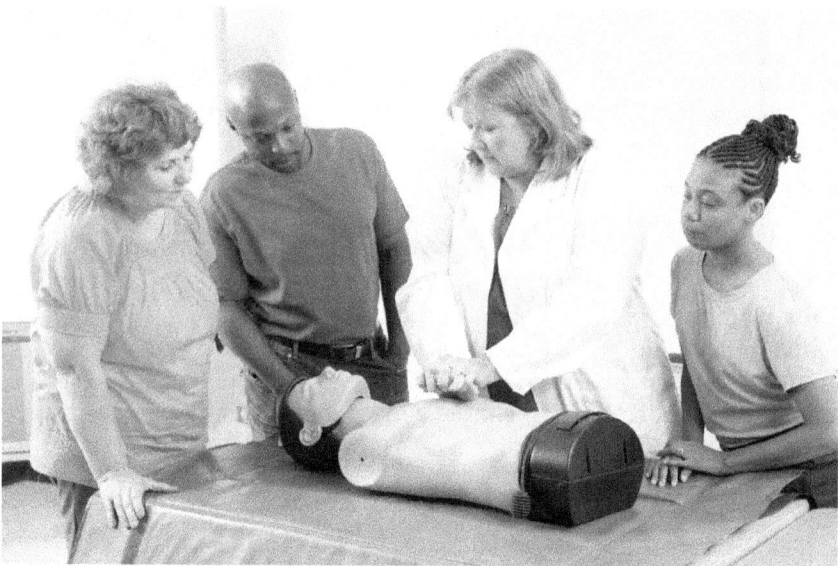

First Aid / CPR

Handling Difficult People

Security officers often find themselves in situations where they must deal with angry people for various reasons. This course will teach officers the basic knowledge of human psychology and a solid set of communication skills. It will also teach officers ways to diffuse a situation with an angry person or deal with difficult people in general.

Work Place Violence

- Detecting Unusual Behavior / Warning Signs
- Anger Management
- Valuing Diversity
- Reporting

Chemical Agents

- Tear Gas and Use of Force
- Pepper Spray Use and Effects
- Airborne Chemical Agents
- Waterborne Chemical Agents

Preserving the Incident Scene

Crowd Control

This gives security officers knowledge in dealing with and controlling crowds. Knowledge will be gained in areas such as: security barriers, directing traffic, the power of words, body language, identifying gang affiliates, recognizing aggression, subduing altercations, escorting unruly individuals, and dispersing the crowd. If needed, security officers will be able to utilize their training and experience to control any situation.

Driver Safety

- Automobiles
- Bicycles
- Golf Carts
- Segway's

Supervision

This course is geared towards improving the leadership skills and operational practices of both new and veteran Security Supervisors. It focuses on leadership, professional standards, setting an example, using communications, customer service and prioritization, risk management, and emergency crisis management.

Some training will be unique to certain environments where incidents are likely to occur or have occurred. This training will prove invaluable while carrying out your daily assignments. If working in the following environments, you will likely receive the following training.

Workplace Security Training

- Hate Crimes
- Bomb Threats
- Building Searches
- Defusing Conflict and Crises
- Diversity Awareness and Sexual Harassment
- Emergency Situations
- Fire Protection and Life Safety
- High-Rise Evacuations

Campus Security Officers Training

- Alcohol Abuse on Campus
- Campus and Community Relations
- Campus Awareness and Crime Prevention
- Critical Incident Response in the School Environment
- Legal Responsibilities
- Residence Hall Security
- Special Events

Hospital Security Officers Training

- Access Control

- Aggressive Behavior
  - Bloodborne Pathogens
  - Defensive Techniques
  - Drug Diversion
  - Fire Apparatus & Response
  - Fitness for Duty
  - High-Rise Building Security
  - Hostage Situation in the Healthcare Setting
  - Infant Abduction
  - Loss Prevention

Shopping Centers Security Training

- Juveniles and Gangs
- Handling Shoplifters
- Legal Responsibilities
- Patrol Operations
- Emergency Response
- Crime Scene Responsibilities

<u>Officers carrying weapons will be trained in the following areas.</u>

Courtroom Demeanor
Parking / Traffic Control
Radio Procedures
Certified Course in Firearms Training
Certified Course in Baton Training
School Security Guard Training
Introduction to Executive Protection
Annual Firearms Requalification
Fire Safety Course

Most security officers must be trained in CPR/First-Aid, so the next few pages will serve as a reminder and checklist of this procedure.

These charts are a guide only and are not a substitute for official training In resuscitation.

INFANT / CHILD CHOKING
LEARN AND PRACTICE CPR (CARDIOPULMANORY RESUSCITATION)
IF ALONE WITH A CHILD WHO IS CHOKING...
1. SHOUT FOR HELP 2. START RESCUE EFFORTS 3. CALL 911 OR LOCAL MEDICAL NUMBER

YOU SHOULD START FIRST-AID IF......	DO NOT START FIRST-AID FOR CHOKING IF....
• The child cannot breathe at all (the chest is not moving up and down). • The child cannot cough, talk, or look blue. • The child is found unconscious. (Go to CPR)	• Child can breathe, talk or cry • Child can cough, sputter, or move air at all. The child's normal reflexes are working to clear the airway. Stand by and encourage coughing.

FIRST-AID

INFANT CPR (0-1 YEARS)	CHILD (1-8 YEARS)
- Give 5 back slaps - Give 2 chest thrusts Alternate slaps and thrusts until the object is dislodged or infant becomes unconscious. If infant becomes unconscious, begin CPR	- Give 5 abdominal thrusts Give thrust with enough force to produce an artificial cough designed to relieve airway obstruction. If child becomes unconscious, begin CPR.

INFANT / CHILD CPR

INFANT CPR (0-1 YEARS)	CHILD CPR (1-8 YEARS)
DO NOT tilt head Give 2 breaths (puffs) Start compressions using **Two fingers only** – 30 times Repeat – 2 breaths, 30 compressions	Tilt head Give 2 full breaths Start compressions Using one or two hands - 30 times Repeat – 2 breaths, 30 compressions

If at any time an object is coughed up and/or infant/child starts to breathe, call 911 or your local emergency number.

ADULT CHOKING
LEARN AND PRACTICE CPR (CARDIOPULMANORY RESUSCITATION)
AFTER CHECKING THE SCENE AND THE INJURED OR ILL PERSON, HAVE SOMEONE CALL 9-1-1 AND GET CONSENT

YOU SHOULD START FIRST-AID IF....	DO NOT START FIRST-AID FOR CHOKING IF....
• The person cannot cough, speak or breathe • The chest does not rise with rescue breaths • The person becomes unconscious Begin CPR	• Person can cough, speak or breathe **Encourage person to continue forcefully coughing.**

FIRST-AID

- Give 5 back blows (between shoulder blades with heel of one hand
- Give 5 abdominal thrusts (place fist with thumb side against middle of persons abdomen, above navel, cover fist w/hand, give 5 upward thrusts)

Alternate blows and thrusts until the object is dislodged, person can cough forcefully, breathe, or until person becomes unconscious. If person becomes unconscious, call 9-1-1 and care for victim.

INFANT / CHILD CPR

Tilt the head and
- Give 1 rescue breath
- (1) Give 30 chest compressions
- (2) Look for and remove object if seen
- (3) Give 2 rescue breaths

Repeat process 1-3

If at any time an object is coughed up and/or infant/child starts to breathe, call 911 or your local emergency number.

Cardio Pulmonary

at a glance

 Check for Danger

 Call for Help
000

 If No Signs of Life
give CPR

①	②	③
Check Response **C**an you hear me? **O**pen your eyes? **W**hat's your name? **S**queeze my hand?	**Establish an airway** Support the jaw and tilt the head. If you see fluid or foreign objects, turn the casualty onto their side and clear	**Check for Breathing** **Look** at the chest **Listen** for air escaping **Feel** for air escaping and chest rising

When you call 911

The Operator will ask the service you require,
Your location and the state you are in.
Ask for an Ambulance
You will be asked:
- The location of the Incident
- The Call Back Phone Number
- Details of the Incident
- If the Casualty is Conscious
- If the Casualty is Breathing
- The Casualty's exact Injury or Illness

The Communications Officer will then make you aware of the actions you should take until paramedics arrive.

Adult CPR

Tilt head
Give 2 full breaths
Start compressions
Using both hands – 30 times
Repeat – 2 breaths,
        30 compressions
Continue until the ambulance arrives, patient recovers or it is impossible to continue

Resuscitation

Signs of life
- **Moving**
- **Conscious**
- **Responsive**
- **Breathing normally**

Remember: Any Attempt at Resuscitation is better than no attempt at all

④	⑤	⑥	⑦
If no breathing, give 2 rescue breaths	**If still no signs of life** Give 30 compressions On the center of the Chest and two rescue breaths. Do this at least 5 times in 2 minutes	**If the person shows signs of life, then place the person on their side**	**Continue until help arrives** If available, implement a defibrillator as soon as possible

Child CPR (1-8 years)
Tilt head
Give 2 full breaths
Start compressions
Using one or two hands
- 30 times
Repeat – 2 breaths,
      30 compressions
Continue until the ambulance arrives, patient recovers or it is impossible to continue

Infant CPR (0-1 years)
DO NOT tilt head
Give 2 breaths (puffs)
Start compressions using
Two fingers only – 30 times
Repeat – 2 breaths,
      30 compressions
Continue until the ambulance arrives, patient recovers or it is impossible to continue

Roy Wyatt

CHAPTER 5
THE CLIENT

Learning objectives

After reading this chapter, you should be able to

- Define Clients and their responsibilities.

- Identify Client expectations of Security personnel.

- Define the key to customer service.

- Identity Client authorities.

- Understand how too much client engagement can be perceived.

- Understand why Security personnel perform non-security-related duties.

THE CLIENT

CHAPTER 5
THE CLIENT

Private security companies are businesses that provide armed and unarmed security services and expertise to private and public clients. Clients are the people who request the services of security firms and/or act on the company's behalf and have the responsibility to oversee the security operations. Depending on the company, this authority is sometimes delegated to their on-site representative or Point of Contact (POC) where the service is actually performed, but not always. Some clients' Points of Contact (POC) can also be out of state.

When providing security, it's important to know who the Point of Contact is. Often, it may be a Regional Manager, Operations Manager, or Director. It doesn't matter as long as you know and can recognize them.

> Define Clients

From a security standpoint, the POC is usually labelled the Client. They have overall responsibility for the security department. For instance, Wells Fargo Bank contracted JJ's Security Services to provide security, so Wells Fargo is the Client. The point of contact is possibly the Branch Manager.

To security, everyone who works on the client's property should be treated as such. Whether the POC is on-site or not, security services are provided to everyone unless informed otherwise.

Clients are the business in any business, especially private security. Without them, there would be no business. Security companies pay, authorize, and/or approve all revenues, and they will go the extra mile to ensure client satisfaction and accommodation. A security company that wants to grow consistently and receive repeat business must be able to retain clients. This will largely depend on the effort the security company is willing to put forth.

The relationship that the security company will be able to establish with the client, along with consistent and constant communication and responsiveness, will prove invaluable in contributing to the retention of existing clients.

Fostering a relationship with the client is critical. To do so, clients should have 24/7 access to a manager in the contracting company. This will be a valuable resource in performing duties and ensuring client satisfaction. As a result, most security firms will assign a manager to every account.

■ Client Expectations

Appearance, responsiveness, frequent communication, covered posts, properly trained officers, and excellent customer service skills are just a few of the Client's expectations. Therefore, clients will appreciate companies that display these characteristics. With these, they will not decide to change Security Companies lightly, even if another competitor offered a lower premium. If clients are satisfied with the current provider, retaining the current services will maximize returns in the long run.

> **THINK ABOUT IT**
> Why are clients so important to security providers?

A good Security Company will receive a majority of new business from existing clients or referrals. For this reason, it is of utmost importance for security officers to fully understand and be able to execute the services for which they have been hired. Regardless of your work location, written instructions for the job duties and expectations should be available. They may be called Post Orders, Operations Procedures manual, etc. Whatever they are, ensure you read, understand, and execute.

Client satisfaction is the ultimate goal of the security company. An officer who does not fit the mold will directly impact clients' perceptions of the security company. Security is ultimately judged by its officers. A professional security officer must understand this and conduct themselves accordingly at all times.

Here are a few expectations from the client. DO NOT TAKE THEM FOR GRANTED.

Look the Part

Clients expect Officers to look professional in their uniforms, which are usually dictated by the Client. Security Officers represent not only the Security Company but also the Client's business. They are the face of clients' businesses and are expected to look professional and perform their jobs to a standard.

It is not the Client's responsibility to inform security personnel of their appearance. If needed, Clients won't approach the officer directly. Instead, whenever they notice an officer's appearance below standard, they will inform the on-duty supervisor or the Manager of

> It is every security officers responsibility to ensure they are adhering to the company's uniform and appearance standards.

the account. If an officer's appearance is a concern, on-site leaders should address these issues.

Clients are very aware of the image officer's project even without saying it. Once they verbalize it, it's oftentimes too late, and their opinion has already been formulated. Remember, you only get one chance to make a first impression. Besides, it's every Security Officers responsibility to ensure they are adhering to the company's uniform and appearance policy. Not the clients.

Be properly Trained

On-site training is essential for the security guard to master the client's site, which is to be protected and secured. Proper on-site training from the security guard supervisors and/or the clients is essential to successful security guard operations.

Initial Training

Many clients will pay for training during the initial training period, sometimes at a lower rate, but not always. Which training will be outlined in the security contract? Security personnel must be adequately trained before working alone on client sites. If not performed by a trainer, newly hired officers will be trained by other security personnel already performing the jobs. During the

> Proper training, without a doubt, improves a security officer's credentials and credibility as a professional. Of course, training aims at employees performing at a level in alignment with the goals and objectives of the organization and its security operation.

initial training period, new hires should bring a pen and a pad, take notes, and ask plenty of questions if necessary. They must be fully prepared before going it alone.

Site duties and responsibilities will dictate the training and number of hours security personnel receive. Depending on the job's difficulty, training can take anywhere from a few hours to several weeks or longer.

During the initial training period, new hires may not learn everything needed. This training is often designed to give officers a general understanding of the jobs so that they can perform them with minimal supervision. The remainder will likely be on-the-job training, especially if they're not working alone.

Training for every scenario is impossible, so sometimes learning will come by trial and error. Security professionals should have good judgment skills and not try and perform something without being adequately trained. If you encounter a unique situation, do not hesitate to notify your Supervisor. It's always best to be sure. Avoid guessing and possibly getting a critical procedure wrong. The critical nature of some jobs can devastate the client services if a procedure is missed or done incorrectly. Company policies and procedures are set in place for a reason. Security personnel's jobs and contracts depend on it.

Security officer with hand outstretched stopping traffic

Have good customer skills

Being a security officer doesn't always mean looking serious. However, security officers must also be friendly. There's nothing like an upset customer speaking to a security officer with little to no customer service skills. Many businesses lose clientele this way.

Security officers will likely interact with customers from time to time, and how they respond and conduct themselves makes a world of difference in their treatment and perception of others. They must always take time to sharpen their customer service skills whenever they can.

Security officers often become the face of many businesses and services. They must be well-versed in customer service, whether they're securing a hospital, stationed at a lobby desk, directing parking, checking identification, patrolling buildings, or providing direction and controlling access.

Most security providers understand the importance of having good customer service skills. Some companies have made the training a requirement. The level of this cannot be underestimated. Customer service is a critical skill, especially in the Security Industry.

While a security officer's primary duty is to protect people, property, information, and reputation, today's security officers also provide a unique level of customer service to help create a safe, engaging, and inviting environment. To do this, security professionals must be friendly, approachable, and enjoy working with the public.

Have good judgment

We all respect good judgment. You can't argue that having and exercising good judgment regularly is essential to success.

Michael Angier wrote it best. He said good judgment comes from experience. And experience often comes from—yup, you guessed it—bad judgment.

Improving our judgment only through experience is expensive, time-consuming, and often heartbreaking. Experience may be a good teacher, but it's not a very efficient one.

> The key to good **customer service** is building good relationships with your customers. Thanking the customer and promoting a positive, helpful and friendly environment will ensure they leave with a great impression. A happy customer will return often and is likely to spend more.

It's far better to learn from the experience of others. If you can trust the advice you receive, and then follow it, you can save yourself a lot of time and pain.

Security is a valued commodity that clients put their faith in to ensure protocols are followed and good judgment is used, especially while away. Discerning the proper response and notification procedures will be vital. Good judgment must always be exercised in the daily performance of duties.

Whenever possible, never substitute the good advice of successful, respected people with your own trial and error. Learn from those who have succeeded. You don't need to follow in their path, but you can travel your unique path with the wisdom and knowledge of those who have gone before. Good judgment is wisdom, and it comes with listening, watching, and learning.

> Never substitute good advice of successful, respected people with your own trial and error. Learn from those who have succeeded.

Follow Directions / Instructions

Becoming a Security Officer means that a large part of your duties and responsibilities will often involve following instructions—verbally or in writing. You must be able to clearly articulate the directions of others and any site-specific procedures.

Clients and your team members will expect you to follow instructions in accomplishing the goal(s) for the account you are working on. These instructions will often be in Site Procedure manuals, but can come from your Supervisor, co-workers, and/or the Client. Rest assured, they are put in place for a reason. Any deviation may need to be approved by the Client and/or Supervisor in some instances.

■ Client's Authority and Responsibilities

Clients are usually aware of how the security department impacts their business and will often look for avenues to improve the operation's overall efficiency. Some will take a more hands-on approach and interact with the security staff, while others are more laid-back. Regarding security, their responsibility is not only to ensure all contract requirements are met, but also to ensure that security officers hired represent their best interest and perform the duties as required per contract.

In private security, clients pull all the strings and exercise their authority as deemed appropriate to accomplish their objectives. Some of their authorities may include:

- oversee security operations;
- set requirements for officers' conduct and training;
- request immediate removal of an officer;
- request additional/change contract hours, and
- add, change, or modify site procedures.

Clients are usually very focused, and decision-making comes from seeing the big picture. In doing so, they often utilize the talent of the staff, Supervisors and Managers.

■ Working With Clients

Because some Clients have additional responsibilities, much of the communication directed will often result from concerns. This doesn't speak for all, as some may be more hands-on, but for the ones who do not have the time to invest, they will often lean more on representatives for information.

> Identify some Client responsibilities?

Clients who invest the time without micro-managing the security department often have a better relationship and perspective of the overall security operations. They are much more in tune with the daily performance of duties and understand the challenges faced on a daily basis.

Even though some clients may not interact much with the officers, rest assured that not much happens without their informed consent.

Whenever clients address any concerns to the security department, they should be corrected as soon as possible. Clients expect issues to be resolved and do not make excuses. They are results-oriented, and a lot of their time should not be taken away for security-related matters. Security-related matters are the responsibility of the security Supervisor(s) and Manager.

Communication

Unless you work in a remote location alone, most Clients' communication will involve the Managers and/or Supervisors. Since they are officers' first-line Supervisors, they will be responsible for the daily operation of the site.

> Clients, who invest the time without micro-managing the security department, oftentimes have a better relationship and perspective of the overall security operations.

Just as the Client will usually go through the Manager or Supervisor, so should the Officers when attempting to communicate with the Client (on security-related matters). When security officers must communicate with the client, the information should be brought to their supervisor, if available. All officers are encouraged to follow their chain of command to get issues resolved, and most of the time, they will resolve them. Any security-related matter must be handled through your security chain of command. Clients are not in the Security Officer's chain of command.

This will change for clients who engage more with the security department. Security officers will appear more comfortable engaging with clients, but I would encourage officers to be mindful of this communication. Any constant communication may appear overfamiliar, which could be misconstrued by other co-workers. This perception oftentimes leads others to suspect any dealings will be unfair without necessarily being accurate. This can also lead other co-workers to feel the following.

- They work for the Client and not the Security Company.
- It's okay to disregard their Supervisor or Manager.
- They feel empowered as a result of familiarity.
- It's okay to disrespect other co-workers.
- They can do whatever they want without any consequences.

In most circumstances, this probably won't be the case, but I have witnessed these actions. Although the outcome may take longer, it usually jeopardizes the officer's job if actions persist.

It is human nature to engage in conversation with people. We are all attracted to certain personalities that make conversation more deliberate and natural. Just be

Be cautious in your communication. Understand that although you work at the Client's site, the Security Company is your employer, and you are responsible for both.

■ Performing Non-Security Related Duties

Professional Security was written to provide security officers with the necessary guidance in becoming professional Security officers and upgrading professionalism within the industry. Unfortunately, many security officers work for organizations where they are required to perform duties that have nothing to do with security. I have often been asked about this, and believe me, it's not as simple as it appears.

> Define the main reason why security perform non-security related duties?

I once managed a site with about twenty security officers. This was a twenty-four-hour site, and three officers worked each shift daily. This was a contract where Clients frequently traveled out of town to conferences. On a weekly basis, a Security Officer was required to drop off employees at the airport, not just the Management, but every level of employees. Whenever a company employee had to leave their vehicle on site, Security was responsible for driving the patrol vehicle and dropping this employee off.

When these types of duties are performed, it's extremely difficult to upgrade the security department's image. So now lies the question of how best to remove these mundane duties or transfer them to another department.

If you were to search the United States for the most ridiculous non-security job duties performed, the entries would be very long and quite humorous. Although there are reasons why these duties have been passed down to security, in a large and broad sense, the primary reason why Security Officers perform non-security related duties is that someone other than a true professional was given the responsibilities to manage or supervise the security department. While this person was well-intentioned, they didn't understand the daily security functions. And what's worse, they may have preconceived notions that are totally inconsistent with projecting a professional security image.

Consider this: would it make sense to have the accounting supervisor responsible for maintenance? Or would it make sense to have the Human Resources Manager responsible for the engineering department?

It's also extremely difficult to remove these duties, and in most instances, it ends up backfiring. Unless the duties are so obsolete that no one would assume the responsibility or notice if they were not performed, it would be very difficult to remove these responsibilities from security.

In your attempt, it's always best to have a plan. You will likely run into a brick wall, but if you have done your homework, it can be done. Start by asking yourself these basic questions:

1. If no one performed the service, what would happen? Think about the impact the service has on the mission. If it can be done without, you have a better argument for eliminating it.

2. If Security no longer performs the service, who will provide it? Is there another department that could take it over? Do your homework. Look for other ideas for possibly having someone else do it.

3. Who needs the service? Someone is benefiting from the service and is ultimately responsible. This is a very important question that will likely get you an answer rather quickly.

It's always best to provide solutions rather than more questions. Clients are usually more willing to listen to suggestions, and ones with solutions usually work pretty well.

SUMMARY

- **Clients** are the people who request the services of security firms.

- **Point-of-Contact acts on behalf of the Company and is** granted the authority to oversee security operations.

- Some **Client expectations** of Security include:
  - Officers must look the Part
  - Be properly trained
  - Have good Customer Service skills
  - Have good Judgment Skills
  - Follow Directions / Instructions

- Some of the **client's authority** consists of:
  - Oversee security operations
  - Set requirements for security, conduct, and training
  - Request immediate removal of an officer
  - Request additional/change contract hours
  - Add, change, or modify site procedures

- **Too much communication** between clients/security officers can have an adverse effect. This can lead the officer(s) to believe:
  - They work for the Client and not the Security Provider
  - It's okay to disregard their Supervisor or Manager of the Account
  - They feel empowered
  - It's okay to disrespect co-workers
  - They can do whatever without consequences
  -

- The primary reason Security Officers **perform non-security related duties** is that someone other than a true professional was responsible for managing or supervising the security department.

CHAPTER 6
SECURITY POSTS / POSITIONS

Officers that work at commercial airports are members of the Transportation Security Administration (TSA) which is controlled by the U.S. Department of Homeland Security. Their main goal is to prevent unauthorized access to restricted areas.

Roy Wyatt

SECURITY POSTS / POSITIONS

CHAPTER 6
SECURITY POSTS / POSITIONS

As you start your quest for information about working in the security guard industry, you'll quickly learn that many different types of security guard jobs exist. It is important that you learn about each type of position to find a security job that is right for you. Even within the same type of security guard position, your specific job responsibilities could vary from employer to employer. It is not only very important that you learn about the different types of security jobs, but you must also read each job description in detail to make sure you are a good fit for the specific job you are considering applying for.

Role and Posts

As a security professional, you will wear many hats, especially as you move up the ladder and work on multiple contracts. In the security industry, the terminology "roles" and "posts" is used to designate many positions. Your *role* refers to your responsibility, whereas a *post* is your work location to carry out that role.

For example, Tom works the loading dock, ensuring all deliveries are properly checked in and merchandise gets to the responsible party. His role is to check in deliveries. His post is the loading dock.

Posts will vary from site to site. And although similar, what's done on one is rarely the same elsewhere. There is no set number of posts on any job site. It can be as few or as many as the job requires.

Security jobs vary in pay and responsibilities. There is sometimes little relationship between the duties performed and compensation. For example, some "Mall Security Officers" who are exposed to serious risk earn less than "Industrial Security Officers" who have less training and responsibility. However, there are now more positions in the security field that separate not just the titles, but the jobs themselves. These roles have progressed, and so have the areas for which security is needed.

Here, you will find a list of roles/posts officers are most likely to work in. This is not at all a conclusive listing, and it will vary depending on the Security Company and the client's needs and expectations. Skillsets and qualifications have also been included.

Lobby Officer

This is a highly visible position that requires an officer to be stationary at a desk or a particular location (usually an entranceway or lobby area) within the client's facility. It requires an officer whose strong suit is customer service—one who has an aptitude for having a great deal of customer contact throughout the day. They are usually the first person everyone sees upon entry and the last before departure.

Your duties will often involve customer service while providing direction to personnel throughout your shift. This Officer will also be skilled at Egress systems, Fire/Life Safety systems, and communication. Additional training will include observation and documentation, dealing with difficult people, and legal aspects and liability.

This position primarily applies to office buildings, campus-style offices, and educational settings.

Some duties and responsibilities may include:

- Providing direction to patrons
- Signing in/out visitors, guests, and contractors
- Notification of clients' contact upon arrival of guests, as well as verification
- Issuing badges
- Familiar with the whereabouts of various functions, agencies, and personnel throughout the day
- Assist customers, employees, and visitors in a courteous and professional manner
- Inspecting the property's personal items
- Enforcing safety
- Foot patrol of interior and exterior areas
- Reporting suspicious behavior
- Enforce rules, regulations, policies, and procedures
- Lock/unlock doors as needed
- Respond to emergencies requiring assistance

Desirable skills and qualifications may include: sharp uniform appearance, good inter-personal and communication skills, good grammar, standing for long periods of time, friendly persona, ability to multi-task, good customer service, telephone etiquette, computer literate, legible handwriting and organized.

Truck Gates and Loading Dock Officer

The main responsibility for these positions is access control, and only authorized and approved personnel will be granted permission to pass through.

Officers working gates have to determine the identity of every person who enters the property. They have to verify that the person is an employee of the company, an expected visitor, or an authorized vendor. At certain complexes, Security Officers should also have documentation on the employees, residents, or visitors who are entering the property.

Depending on the site and the critical nature of products, services, and/or people, this is a very critical position that demands a high-caliber Officer with a great deal of attention to detail and a focus on customer service.

Some duties and responsibilities may include:

- Verify and document everyone before granting access
- Inspection of shipment and/or products
- Providing direction to patrons
- Signing in/out visitors, guests, and contractors
- Notification of clients' contact upon arrival of products
- Issuing badges as needed
- Familiar with the whereabouts of various functions, agencies, and personnel throughout the day
- Provide assistance to customers, employees, and visitors in a courteous and professional manner
- Reporting suspicious behavior
- Enforce rules, regulations, policies, and procedures
- Open/close gates as needed

Desirable skills and qualifications may include: attention to detail, friendly and professional demeanor, good listening skills, computer literate, legible handwriting, organized, good communicator, good interpersonal skills, strong customer service skills, ability to multi-task, maintain composure when dealing with unusual circumstances and dealing with aggressive behavior.

Patrol Officer (Foot and/or Vehicle)

Patrol operations have always been a critical and large component in any security profession. This enhances security in many ways, including, but not limited to, response times for situations, easily accessible for clients/guests, visible deterrent, etc. Some of them utilize checklists and are also provided with weapons, radios, flashlights, and, in some cases, a wand if your account is set up on a Guard Tour System.

If you're on a Guard Tours System, this requires regular patrols. However, electronic systems have recently risen in popularity due to their lightweight, ease of use, and downloadable logging capabilities.

However, regular patrols are becoming less accepted as an industry standard. They provide predictability for the would-be criminal and monotony for the Security Officer on duty. Random patrols are easily programmed into electronic systems, allowing greater freedom of movement and unpredictability.

In the event of an emergency or incident, rovers are generally the first point of contact in responding, rendering aid, and/or investigating an incident. Patrol Officers must become familiar with the perimeters of the property, including the surrounding area and personnel. Periodic checks around the perimeter, building exit points, and any other area of concern will also be conducted. They may drive or walk from location to location. The Client may request the guard to inspect vehicles for illegal or stolen property as well.

Some duties and responsibilities may include:

- Provide customer assistance in a professional and courteous manner.
- Warn violators of infractions such as smoking, loitering, and carrying forbidden articles.
- Prepares logs or reports as required for the post; writes or types reports or enters information in a computer using standard grammar; inspects security control logs and takes action as required.

- Patrol assigned areas while checking for the following: unauthorized persons, security violations, mechanical problems, hazards, unlocked doors, blocked ingress and egress; inspects buildings and grounds using appropriate equipment and protective gear.
- Observe and report incidents or suspicious activity
- Watch for unusual or irregular conditions that may create security concerns for safety hazards.
- Permit authorized persons to enter the property and monitor entrances and exits

Desirable skills and qualifications may include: possess a valid driver's license, have a High school diploma or equivalent, possess a current security license, standing for long periods of time, ability to multi-task, good verbal and communication skills, very flexible, takes pride in job, customer service oriented, display a positive attitude, exercise discretion, strong moral and ethical character.

- Observe department personnel to protect against theft of company property and ensure that authorized removal of property is conducted within the appropriate client requirements.
- Perform other duties as requested by the client

Patrol Officers must be very knowledgeable in other duties, as they sometimes perform them as well. Besides working closely with the Supervisor, they may also perform certain lobby and access control functions, including verifying visitors and guests, signing in and out of visitors and guests, receiving calls, giving breaks, etc.

Alarm Response Officer

This Officer's responsibility is similar to that of Patrol Officers, with the exception that their duties are more focused on alarm responding. Their primary purpose is to investigate the source of alarms on the Client's premises and troubleshoot the signal. Disturbances such as fires, property damage, faulty equipment, unlawful entry, and vandalism will also be investigated. Any irregularities must be reported to their Supervisor for further instructions. Coordinate activities with Police and Fire Department Officials during alarms.

Some duties and responsibilities may include:

- Coordinate activities with authorities such as Police and/or Emergency personnel
- Prepares logs or reports as required for the post; writes investigation and automobile reports.
- Investigate the source of alarms by responding to various locations
- Troubleshoot alarms

Desirable skills and qualifications may include: possess a valid and clean driver's license, highly motivated, bondable, have a High School diploma or equivalent, possess a current security license, ability to multi-task, good verbal and communication skills, very flexible, takes pride in job, customer service oriented, display a positive attitude, exercise discretion, strong moral and ethical character.

Training Officer/Sargent

Trainers handle the learning and professional development of the company's workforce. While district trainers explain company policy and guidelines to new employees, Site trainers explain the site policies and procedures. Some often write and/or provide them with an employee handbook. Their top priority is to ensure employees have a firm grasp of their job description and what the company and client expect from them.

Training officers instruct employees on aspects such as equipment use, uniform appearance standards, proper procedures, filing procedures, and the proper way to greet customers. Occasionally, training officers will write and distribute a manual to assist the process. They may also have related HR duties and be responsible for handling and explaining paychecks and benefits, motivating employees, and making sure they work as a team.

Some duties and responsibilities may include:

- Select and prepare correspondence relating to training programs
- Supervise the establishment and maintenance of essential training records and files
- Market-specific training booklets and training courses to address all generic and site-specific subjects; obtains approved material to support all required training.
- Provides information briefings and training at the client's request
- Design and develop training courses
- Maintain Instructor certification in CPR/First-Aid, AED, etc., as required by contract
- Scores, inputs, and/or coordinates training levels.
- Inventory, order, and distribute training manuals, exams, awards, and gifts.
- Present any contractual and state-required training
- Flexible in working multiple levels within the organization to identify, analyze, and solve

Desirable skills and qualifications may include: ability to express ideas via spoken words, strong written and verbal communication skills, organized, energetic and passionate about their line of work, has reliable transportation, ability to work a flexible work schedule, ability to get along with employees/customers and clients, have a firm grasp of what the company expects from employees and feel comfortable delegating, training and review officers' performance, requires confidence and professionalism.

problems and create opportunities for continuous improvement.

- Maintain confidentiality of all information and data.

Caretaker Officer

This position usually provides general caretaking and porterage duties, including first-line maintenance of systems and grounds maintenance as required.

Some duties and responsibilities may include:

- Monitor fuel level to ensure stock is maintained
- Maintain equipment and furniture
- Provide first-line response to general equipment failures and undertake repairs where possible.
- First-line repair and maintenance of fixtures and fittings, H&S checks and recording, including testing of lighting, heating, and alarm systems, emergency generators, and boiler plant.
- Preparing venues for meetings, conferences, and special events, including providing and clearing equipment, drinks, etc.
- Monitor daily consumable stocks as required, such as custody supplies, light tubes, and laundry sorting, to ensure a high level of service is maintained.
- Collect and prepare waste for disposal, including transportation where required. Operate and maintain the shredding machine where required.
- In the absence of cleaning staff, assist with cleaning where needed
- Perform grounds maintenance and keep the building surroundings clean and tidy, including washing cars, snow removal, keeping paths and walkways clear, etc.
- Perform mail room and general courier duties as required to ensure a smooth-running courier and driving service. Courier duties will include the transportation of prisoners, personnel, mail, equipment, property, confidential waste, and scrap to various locations. Collect and deliver Police vehicles to enable maintenance events to be carried out and perform any other driving duties.

Desirable skills and qualifications may include: experience of caretaking and grounds maintenance, experience and communication skills – written and verbal, computer skills, good organizational skills – able to plan, prioritize and coordinate activities, problem solving ability, self-motivated, and focused on achieving high levels of performance, able to balance conflicting demands, with a willing, flexible and adaptable approach, physically fit and able to undertake manual handling and other physical requirements of the post.

- Conducting checks and routine maintenance of property vehicles.
-

Security Coordinator

According to a Salary.com job summary, a security coordinator "coordinates, develops, and evaluates security programs for an organization. " They ensure programs are effective and identify the need for additional resources, such as an increased number of security guards at a particular location or within an organization or business.

They work in various locations, from corporate offices to residential buildings, hospitals, municipal buildings, and entertainment and gaming venues. They oversee security functions within any of these organizations, and their profession is much more commonly located in metropolitan areas, according to the U.S. Department of Labor Bureau of Labor Statistics. They must be familiar with all government regulations and good industry practice.

Some duties and responsibilities may include:

- Coordinate monthly Security Monitor duty schedules
- Assist with the implementation of system-wide security staff training and follow-up training for Security Monitors. This includes, but is not limited to, training on security booth operations and policies, writing incident reports, and emergency procedures.
- Conducting a system walk-through with new users to determine that all functions are operating correctly.
- Annual self-certification of campus compliance with the applicable information
- Determining users' access to reports, as well as each reporting file, and the available fields within each file.
- Signing and overseeing the completion and submission of the appropriate access forms.
- Preparing for the implementation of a compliant security awareness program for delivering online.
- Assisting with various annual risk assessments and penetration test reviews.
- Manage a project to introduce laptop encryption.
- Perform other duties as required in development and administration.
- Maintain consistent accountability for fulfilling the Security Monitor role, including setting clear expectations for performance and providing rationale for policies and procedures.
- Assist in the management of payroll operations, which includes, but is not limited to, entering weekly work schedules into the system, daily verifications of both scheduled and hours worked, and timely reporting of payroll issues.
- Plan and facilitate Security staff meetings

Desirable skills and qualifications may include: bachelor's degree in computer science or related field, familiar with penetration and vulnerability assessment, possess a valid and clean driver's license, security licensed, excellent interpersonal skills, detailed and results oriented, report writing experience, supervisory experience, video surveillance, good leadership skills, good verbal and communication skills, knowledge of virus protection methods and encryption techniques, very flexible, team player, accepts responsibility, creating schedules, fire alarm systems, takes pride in job, knowledge of data security models – methodologies and techniques, customer service oriented, proficient in Microsoft Officer software, conflict resolution skills, exercise discretion, strong moral and ethical character.

Detention or Correction Officer

These officers are responsible for the safety and security of transporting, guarding, and escorting detainees from one location to another. Their primary duties will include, but not be limited to, armed transportation services, escorting detainees to and from transport vehicles, and monitoring detainees in your custody.

Some security companies provide services to nuclear power plants, oil and gas companies, airports, ports, banks, hospitals, factories, warehouses, commercial facilities, residential communities, and more.

Some duties and responsibilities may include:

- Inspect and prepare transportation vehicles for daily operation requirements; perform pre- and post-trip inspection of vehicles; fill out required paperwork to report any damage or defects
- Conduct pat-down searches of detainees; ensure that detainees are properly secured prior to leaving a facility and while in a vehicle; ensure that all paperwork is obtained and completely accurate and thorough when obtaining detainees at a facility and delivering them to their appropriate destinations
- Safe operation of vehicles; ensures that all safety and legal measures are followed at all times while transporting detainees, including but not limited to all federal, state, municipal, and organizational laws, regulations, policies, and procedures
- Exercise of good judgment, courage, alertness, even temperament, and ability to render satisfactory performance through knowledge of his/her position responsibilities.

Desirable skills and qualifications may include: ability to meet and maintain any applicable licensing, including driver's license or certification requirements, current or valid license, specific experience required, driving experience, civilian or military law enforcement, experience as a security officer engaged in functions related to detaining civil or administrative detainees, experience in dealing tactfully with the general public, capability of understanding and applying written and verbal orders, rules and regulations, ability to interpret printed rules and regulations, detailed written orders, training instructions and materials, ability to compose reports, maintain poise and self-control during situations such as: fires, evacuations, disturbances and explosions, operate radio/telephone equipment, monitor console, assess and evaluate situations effectively, identify critical issues accurately and detail oriented.

Command/Control Center Operator

These highly skilled operators report directly to the Supervisor and/or Manager of the account. On some accounts, Supervisors perform these functions.

Command Center Operators undergo an extensive training program that covers areas such as alarm response, fire/life safety, emergency response, and CCTV monitoring and reviewing. They can either be stationed at the building they are monitoring or at a remote location.

These Operators protect the company's assets by monitoring alarm systems and paging emergency personnel when needed. They are part of a team within the central alarm monitoring station that monitors and responds to signals received from alarm and access control systems.

Their training and responsibilities generally require them to be compensated more as well.

Some duties and responsibilities may include:

- Processes various alarm events in accordance with standard operating procedures.
- Ensures customers and responding parties are accurately informed of the situation in a timely fashion and updated on any amplifying information.
- Control access to the client facility; assists visitors with a legitimate need to gain entry into the facility
- Representative will efficiently ask appropriate questions and analyze the course of action required in a calm and controlled manner
- Enters information into the security monitoring and dispatch system.
- Monitors entrances and exits; prevents unapproved or unlawful entry; controls entrances, the movement of people and vehicles, and parking
- Coordinate police, fire, ambulance, and other emergency requests,

- Answers or forwards nonemergency requests for assistance.
- Communicates in a manner that is open, honest, and responsive in all situations; to the extent authorized, provides information regarding the facility and surrounding area as requested by visitors.
- Supervises shift to ensure that all requests and alarms are being handled correctly and in a timely manner
- Test communications and alarm equipment

Desirable skills and qualifications may include: supervisory experience, pleasant speaking voice w/clear tone, alarm monitoring, keyboarding skills, technical knowledge, computer skills, some college, call center experience, strong customer service, ability to multi-task, strong organizational skills, high level success within a team, communicates professionally, neat and professional appearance, ability to maintain professional composure when dealing with unusual circumstances, detailed oriented, and presents a good image of the client and security.

- Processing inbound calls in a manner that provides courteous and professional service, which includes, but is not limited to, resolving customer calls in relation to technical matters
- Will provide basic data entry and administration support as needed.
- Reviews and ensures reports are written for all incidents on his/her shift
- Preserves order and may enforce regulations pertaining to personnel, visitors, and premises.

Custom Protection Officer

These are primarily courtesy patrol officers who are usually hired to man residential complexes, apartment buildings, gated communities, and homeowner associations. In most instances, a CPO carries similar rights to a Police Officer but is limited by location.

These officers' scope of duties is focused on providing assistance to the residents of each community they serve. They must work with clients to maintain a positive image of the property served and provide an overall positive experience for tenants and their guests.

They are highly trained and mostly armed, depending on the contracts agreed upon with clientele. They are more likely to interact with the general public and confront the criminal element. The employees tend to take pride in the title "Security Officer" or "Protection Officer" and disdain the label of "guard."

Some duties and responsibilities may include:

- Perform security patrols of designated areas on foot or in a vehicle

- Watch for irregular or unusual conditions that may create security concerns or safety hazards
- Sound alarms or call the police or the fire department in case of fire or the presence of unauthorized persons
- Warn violators of rule infractions, such as loitering, smoking, or carrying forbidden articles
- Permit authorized persons to enter the property and monitor entrances and exits
- Issue citations in accordance with policies and procedures
- Observe departing personnel to protect against theft of company property and ensure that authorized removal of property is conducted within the appropriate client requirements
- Investigate and prepare reports on accidents, incidents, and suspicious activities
- Provide assistance to customers, employees, and visitors in a courteous and professional manner
- Manage multiple teams of Security Officers, Site and Shift Supervisors in the Operations Manager's absence, including hiring/selection, scheduling, data entry, payroll, training, coaching, development, and support.
- Build, improve, and maintain effective relationships with both clients and employees.
- Conducting inspections of designated accounts as per schedule and providing documentation required by the Operations Manager.
- Handle any escalated security issues or emergency situations appropriately

Desirable skills and qualifications may include: must be able to pass any state-required training or other qualifications for licensing, pass a state licensing test if driving a company-owned or client-provided vehicle, law enforcement experience, service in the elite military forces, military police or combat arms, graduate of police/corrections academy, criminal justice degree, associate or higher, career military, ability to operate radio or telephone equipment and/or console monitors, ability to interact cordially and communicate with the public, effective oral and written communication skills, active listening skills, ability to assess and evaluate situations effectively, ability to identify critical issues quickly and accurately and attention to detail.

Special Event Officer

Special event security officers patrol the grounds of special events. Their primary responsibility is protecting against terrorism, theft, and other illegal activities. They also observe special event attendees to ensure that they are abiding by the venue's laws and rules. According to eHow Contributor, these officers may work at sporting events, stadiums, theaters, concerts, conventions, ballrooms, parties, or other large events.

Special event security officers usually complete training sponsored by the employer prior to the event.

Depending on the site and the critical nature of products, services, and/or people, this is a very critical position that demands a high-caliber officer with a great deal of attention to detail, a customer service focus, interpersonal and communication skills, and a very security-conscious.

Due to an increase in crime rates, such as material robbery and data theft, effective security measures are certainly needed. Security officers provide their services in a wide range of facilities, such as public places, private bungalows, government offices, private business facilities, entertainment settings, and many others. Accordingly, their duties are typically determined by where they are working.

Some duties and responsibilities may include:

- Being stationed at various posts throughout the event
- Patrol the grounds of the event on foot or in a vehicle
- Check attendees' tickets or credentials
- Work closely with other staff members
- Search bags or other belongings brought into the venue.
- Assist customers with special needs, such as retrieving wheelchairs
- Ticket taking and/or monitoring the door
- Monitor surveillance equipment to ensure compliance
- Watch for irregular or unusual conditions that may create security concerns or safety hazards
- Detain anyone violating venue rules/regulations
- Perform crowd control
- Direct traffic and/or control parking
- Intervene when problems arise

> ***Desirable skills and qualifications may include:*** standing for long periods of time, working a flexible schedule, good driving record, ability to operate radio or telephone equipment, monitor cameras of events activity, ability to interact cordially and communicate with the public, effective oral and written communication skills, active listening skills, ability to assess and evaluate situations effectively, following directions, ability to identify critical issues quickly and accurately, attention to detail, working in unusual conditions and vigilant in looking for threats or hazards.

Transportation / Airport Security Officer

Officers who work at commercial airports are members of the Transportation Security Administration (TSA), which is controlled by the U.S. Department of Homeland Security.

Their main goal is to prevent unauthorized access to restricted areas. They are responsible for security in commercial airports, which involves duties such as checking travel baggage as it passes through the scanning machines and examining travelers using hand-held wands.

Many people are attracted to airport security officers. They present an exciting opportunity to protect our nation and keep the skies safe. Furthermore, for anyone interested in aviation, they provide an opportunity to constantly be around planes and airports.

These security officers work in airport check-in sections, as well as in security, parking, air cargo operations, and ground transportation. Though their work is typically routine, it can require long hours and be very dangerous.

Some duties and responsibilities may include:

- Ability to work with people of diverse backgrounds
- Provide good customer service
- Physical check objects, persons, and vehicles entering the area assigned
- Operate X-ray machines and hand-held wands at checkpoints
- Communicate non-technical information effectively to others
- Complete written reports
- Checking baggage/individuals
- Ensure proper credentials are on hand
- Continuous efforts to streamline and speed up security process while not compromising safety
- Be familiar with airfield access and direct patrons to proper authorities if needed
- Patrol grounds of event on foot or vehicle
- Check attendees

Desirable skills and qualifications may include: pass a criminal and background check, ability to read/write at a certain level, follow and give clear directions clearly in English, be able to absorb information about airport policies and procedures, standing for long periods of time, attention to detail, monitor and observe behavior, interact cordially and communicate with the public, capable of reporting and correcting infractions, identify and detect suspicious materials, Correcting infractions by giving verbal warning, expelling people or detaining offenders of more serious infractions to authorities and ability to lift objects up to possibly 20-25lbs.

Campus Security Officer

A campus security officer promotes and maintains safety at a college or university by ensuring the safety of students, staff, and faculty, as well as the property. They support the efforts of campus and local police.

They are a uniformed presence that patrols the campus by monitoring behavior, ensuring security of buildings and property, maintaining order, investigating disturbances, and enforcing regulations.

Getting a job as a campus security officer may require additional certifications in CPR, first aid, and firearm use. Some employers also require officers to attend continuing education programs to maintain their certification.

Some duties and responsibilities may include:

- Greet and direct all visitors
- Attend training functions
- Monitor alarm systems
- Make interior and exterior patrols
- Patrol property by mobile, foot, and bicycle
- Tag and/or tow illegally parked vehicles
- Respond to complaints regarding disturbances or security violations
- Ensure areas are locked at night to include libraries, halls, clubhouses, and the pool
- Monitor site lighting and notify maintenance of any outages
- Write reports of any incidents
- Maintain care of personal and department equipment
- Permit only authorized individuals to enter the building
- Perform functions as directed to protect the building and its occupants
- Evaluate, investigate, and report all types of security and law enforcement incidents
- Perform checks of the building and assist faculty, staff, students, and visitors as needed
- Respond to false alarm calls and disarm if needed
- Assist residents with lockouts

Desirable skills and qualifications may include: 1-3 years' experience, appropriate state certification or license, valid driver's license, pass background and drug testing, CPR/first-aid/AED qualified, good communication and observational skills, making good decisions and being strong problem-solvers, good verbal and writing skills, standing and/or walking for long periods of time.

Hospital Security Officer

A hospital security officer looks after the security and safety at public hospitals and private medical facilities. They are trained to specifically manage emergency crises such as fire, drug theft, and other hospital equipment, and criminal actions. They have to check for any illicit activities that can be carried out in hospitals. They also have to handle situations where the relatives of the patients get aggressive with nurses and doctors at times. They even control the hidden security camera systems for checking any doubtful activities in the medical setting.

Desirable skills and qualifications may include: pass a criminal and background check, ability to read/write at a certain level, standing for long periods of time, attention to detail, monitor and observe behavior, interact cordially and communicate with the public, capable of reporting and correcting infractions, identify and detect suspicious behavior, expelling people or detaining offenders of more serious infractions to authorities.

Hospitals present unique challenges for security officers. Many hospitals employ security/safety officers who provide hospital security and protect patients in the event of any criminal activity, fire, or bomb threat. Hospitals have multiple entrances, many vulnerable patients, and medicines that can be stolen and sold illegally.

Some duties and responsibilities may include:

- Patrol the premises, ensuring the hospital is secure and identifying potential security threats
- Keep a watch out for theft by employees and visitors,
- Monitor unauthorized persons and patient safety
- Arresting individuals who are found making trouble
- Monitor cameras to detect any crime and/or illegal activities
- Monitor particular and confidential areas such as: trauma units, infant care, the medicine storage area, the prisoner care area, and the psychiatric ward, guard money drawers, and inventory valuables in the hospital.
- Check for fire hazards
- Testing fire detectors and fire extinguishers
- Ensure emergency exits are clear of obstructions.
- Coordinate evacuations due to a fire or bomb threat
- Operate safety equipment
- Investigate any accidents and document any crimes or problems that jeopardize the safety of the hospital's occupants.
- Sign in hospital visitors

Bank Protection Officer

These professionals make sure that the banking operations in financial houses are carried out smoothly. They keep a close eye on every customer with the intention of preventing fraudulent activities. Typically, they carry guns and other equipment in order to prevent any theft.

This officer ensures everyone who enters the bank has a genuine reason. They are responsible for seeing that all the rules of the banks are adhered to. In case a person is dressed suspiciously, the Bank Security Officer has the right to ask him/her to prove their authentication if such rules are defined by the bank. Their main duty is to make sure they avert crime. For this, they should always be alert and ready for any unwarranted situations or circumstances.

Some duties and responsibilities may include:

- Enforce violations of rule infractions to include: loitering, smoking or carrying forbidden articles.
- Monitor the functioning of bank security surveillance systems.
- Patrols of designated areas on foot or in a vehicle
- If armed, take charge of the situation when confronted with a robbery.
- Watch for irregular or unusual conditions that may create security concerns or safety hazards.
- Effective oral and written communication skills.
- Sound alarms or call the police or the fire department in case of fire or the presence of unauthorized persons.
- Monitors entrances and exits.
- Handle security issues or emergency situations appropriately.
- Investigate and prepare reports on accidents, incidents, and suspicious activities.
- Be aware and familiarize yourself with the site's operational procedures.
- Provide assistance to customers, employees, and visitors in a courteous and professional manner.

Desirable skills and qualifications may include: excellent observation skills, must possess a high school diploma or equivalent, pass any State-required training or other qualifications for licensing, armed license, ability to handle stress and keep a cool head, driving a company-owned or client-provided vehicle, prior military experience, good leadership skills, prior security experience, a good knowledge of first-aid techniques, walking/standing for long periods of time, assess and evaluate situations effectively, neat and professional appearance, attention to detail, ability to interact cordially and communicate with customers, must have reliable transportation, must be team oriented and ability to work independently and monitor consoles CCTV systems.

Mall / Shopping Center Security Officer

Mall security officers may be employed by a single store or the entire shopping center. The basic function of a mall security guard is to protect his employer from theft, vandalism and other illegal activity while maintaining order. Specific job duties vary from position to position. Mall security guards are also referred to as loss prevention agents.

Retail security officers aren't always uniformed; some work undercover in plain clothes to spot possible thieves.

Some use cameras to watch over customers. Either way, they must act swiftly and confidently when dealing with suspicious activity. Retail security officers have to be prepared to use force, particularly when apprehending and detaining shoplifting suspects. Most retail security officers spend a long time on their feet, walking the premises and staying alert.

Many of these Officers are employed part-time, allowing workers to pursue other interests. However, weekend and holiday shifts are common. Security officers may also be asked to work longer hours during peak shopping seasons, including Christmas.

Some duties and responsibilities may include:

- Patrols of designated areas on foot, patrol vehicle, or Segway
- Watch for irregular or unusual conditions that may create security concerns or safety hazards
- Effective oral and written communication skills
- Sound alarms or call the police or the fire department in case of fire or the presence of unauthorized persons
- Warn violators of rule infractions, such as loitering, smoking, or carrying forbidden articles
- Monitor cameras to detect any crime and/or illegal activities
- Operate safety equipment
- Apprehend and/or detain the suspect for shoplifting or illegal behavior

Site / Shift Supervisor

The supervisor is responsible for all aspects of security as outlined in the post orders and reports directly to the account manager.

Site Supervisors are generally in charge of all officers assigned to the account, while Shift Supervisors' responsibilities are limited to their shift of officers. Although officers may seek guidance from any Supervisor, they are encouraged to use their chain of command. Their on-duty Supervisor should be made aware of any issues or concerns first.

Supervisors report directly to the account manager. They supervise the day-to-day activities to ensure policies and procedures are followed and operations run smoothly and effectively. They will address any and all issues and concerns and handle them accordingly.

Supervisors are a valuable commodity in the Security Industry and provide expertise in on-site procedures. Since supervisors work alongside the officers, clients usually interact with them regularly.

Desirable skills and qualifications may include: standing/walking for long periods of time, aware of their surroundings, very customer service oriented, strong communicators, capable of reporting and correcting infractions, able to convey critical information to suspects, employees and law enforcement officials, identify and correct suspicious behavior, confident, professional, assertive when necessary and not easily rattled, expelling people or detaining offenders of more serious infractions to authorities, possess strength and stamina in the event they are forced to chase or restrain a suspect.

Unless the account manager is on-site, Supervisors are often the face of the Security Company and the backbone of holding some accounts together. Apart from the management role, Supervisors also carry out patrols and other security duties themselves.

Some duties and responsibilities may include:

- Responsible for all activities during his/her shift, ensure that his/her shift and/or personnel report and depart within the proper time frames.
- Make every effort to fill a vacancy in the case of a call-off
- If the fill-in arrives late, the shift supervisor must stay to prevent lost time
- Monitor personnel performance while performing assigned tasks
- Directly supervise the activities of his/her personnel
- Assist the Console Operator having problems
- Counsel personnel on performance, attitude, and professionalism
- Responsible for all paperwork generated from his/her shift, which is correct, legible, and filled in.
- Ensure that everyone is rotated appropriately for each position throughout his/her shift

Desirable skills and qualifications may include: excellent people skills, strong leadership skills, demonstrated customer service skills, exemplary professional image and attitude, ability to act as a supervisor versus a friend or 'buddy', maturity, good communication skills, detail oriented and ability to maintain professional composure when dealing with unusual circumstances.

- Ensure that policies and procedures in the post orders are adhered to
- Ensure that personnel are aware of and follow the company's standards of conduct
- Must not show favoritism in the performance of duties and deal with issues diplomatically

- Grant shift exchange requests - the supervisor must keep the exchanges under control to prevent lost time, overtime, and possible confusion of work schedules. When this is granted, the account Manager must be made aware of the date and persons involved
- Assist with conducting orientation and training of all new personnel
- Complete required shift logs and reports. Be compliant with site post orders, Security, and client policies and procedures
- Maintain a standard of image; conduct oneself in a professional, calm, and courteous manner at all times
- Make recommendations for positive and negative personnel actions for those under his/her direct supervision
- Inspect all Officers at the start of each shift for appearance and readiness for duty

Area / Field Supervisor

Field Supervisors can report to an Operations, Account, or District Manager. Although their title is "supervisor," they have similar responsibilities to a Manager and often act with the same authority in their absence. The term "field" in the security industry means they will oversee multiple locations in a particular region.

Their main objective is to assist Operations, District, or Account Managers with supervising the day-to-day security operations of a portfolio of assigned sites.

Desirable skills and qualifications may include: neat and professional appearance, quality customer service, strong leadership and coaching skills, supervisory experience in the security industry, manage multiple priorities and complex situations with a diverse team of employees and client requirements on an ongoing basis, communicate effectively both orally and written, intermediate to advanced computer skills, outstanding impersonal and communications skills, strong management skills, Ability to handle typical and crisis situations efficiently and effectively at the client site.

They should be flexible, focused, and driven while ensuring that policies and procedures are met across the board.

Some duties and responsibilities may include:

- Assist with the start-up of a new business
- Assist with transporting officers to locations and sit post whenever the Operations/Account Manager isn't able to fill the post.
- Inspecting, reporting problems & helping to maintain/deliver equipment (radios, pagers, uniforms, paychecks), etc.
- Manage multiple teams of Security Officers, Site and Shift Supervisors in the Operations Manager's absence, including hiring/selection, scheduling, data entry, payroll, training, coaching, development, and support.
- Build, improve, and maintain effective relationships with both clients and employees.

- Conducting inspections of designated accounts as per schedule and providing documentation required by the Operations Manager.
- Handle any escalated security issues or emergency situations appropriately
- Providing site-specific training to new security officers
- Assist Operations Manager in meeting all the necessary reporting and contract compliance requirements.
- Other management responsibilities as determined by the Clients, Operations Manager(s), or District Manager.

Operations / Field / Area Manager

This Manager is accountable for the day-to-day operations of a portfolio of assigned client sites and the overall operations of these accounts.

Because of the geography and number of accounts, this is a very demanding position that requires dedication, strong leadership, and excellent interpersonal skills.

Supervisors are their greatest assets. Since supervisors will often be their main POC (Point of Contact), having strong leadership in place will prove invaluable. More leadership and delegation have been proven advantages for these managers.

New accounts' start-up will likely be their responsibility as well. Because the infancy stages of new businesses are such a critical time period, the manager's presence and expertise will prove invaluable until the account is up and running.

You must also have a great deal of drive and self-discipline.

Some duties and responsibilities may include:

- Managing, including hiring, training, and enhancing the employee experience of our Security Officers
- Building and maintaining relationships with clients and employees at assigned sites:
- training, developing, and retaining staff

Desirable skills and qualifications may include: College degree, Effective organizational skills, ability to grow business, neat and professional appearance, quality customer service, strong leadership and coaching skills, management experience in the security industry, manage multiple priorities and complex situations with a diverse team of employees and client requirements on an ongoing basis, communicate effectively both orally and written, intermediate to advanced computer skills, outstanding impersonal and communications skills, strong management skills, Ability to handle typical and crisis situations efficiently and at client site.

- Coordinate support and solve problems affecting the account management and service delivery.
- Meeting or exceeding financial, operational, and compliance goals.
- Working with site supervisors and officers to ensure high-quality customer service.
- Oversee and maintain weekly operating schedules and payroll for assigned security personnel.
- Provide after-hours response at client sites on their shift, including site inspections, emergency response, and discipline issues.
- Manage security officers at multiple client locations. Based on a full-time rotating schedule with a broad geography, I am responsible for the security officers on the Field Operations Manager's assigned shift.
- Direct and indirect reports: 50 + security officers, depending on size and number of clients. All site supervisors and Security Officers at sites without a site supervisor will report directly to this position.

Account Mgr., Director of Security, Assignment Manager, Asset Protection Mgr., Operations Mgr., etc.

These Managers oversee security operations for the entire business or account, including training, scheduling, discipline, payroll, hiring, and terminating employees. They develop and enforce security policies to ensure a safe environment for employees and visitors.

They are responsible for the day-to-day operations of the account while building, improving, and maintaining relationships with clients and employees.

They develop and retain staff, coordinate needed support services to run the account effectively, meet or exceed financial and operational goals, and provide quality customer service.

Their uniforms will be dictated depending on the account. Most wear business attire, but it can vary.

Some duties and responsibilities may include:

- Supervise daily security operations of an assigned site.
- Risk management
- Ensuring compliance with local, state, and federal guidelines regarding emergency and security. They also serve as liaisons with local law enforcement to assist investigations of accidents, thefts, and property loss.
- Management includes hiring, training, and coordinating the work schedules of all security personnel to ensure a secure environment at all times.

- Manage a team of Security Officers, Site and Shift Supervisors, including hiring/selection, scheduling, payroll, training, coaching, development, and support
- Ensure the Client Site is provided with high-quality security services to protect people and property
- Build, improve, and maintain effective relationships with both clients and employees
- Coordinate necessary support services to effectively manage the client site to meet or exceed financial and operational goals and provide quality customer service
- Ensure all required reporting and contract compliance requirements are met
- Handle any escalated security issues or emergency situations appropriately
- Other management responsibilities as determined by the Client or District Manager
- Communicate staffing needs via Requisition Form; assist recruiters in identifying, interviewing, and hiring quality candidates.
- Administer site safety programs, workers' compensation, and risk management programs as appropriate to the site and corporate procedures.

Desirable skills and qualifications may include: college degree in business administration/criminal justice or equivalent experience, 3-5 years of security management experience, previous experience working in very diverse customer sites preferred, ability to develop and grow customer relationships, experience in hiring, developing, motivating and retaining staff, strong time management experience required; ability to perform multiple tasks simultaneously, outstanding interpersonal and communications skills required, ability to work in a team-oriented management environment with the ability to work independently, ability to manage multiple priorities, complex situations, a diverse team of employees and client requirements on an ongoing basis, previous payroll, billing and scheduling experience preferred, key competencies: staff management, financial management, integrity, problem solving, conflict management, time management, customer focus, timely decision making, motivating and directing others.

- Prepare/manage the annual budget and meet account financial goals, including gross profit, overtime, and payroll accuracy. High employee retention and low turnover will greatly impact these.
- Perform account audits and off-hour visits, completing required documentation.
- Manage uniforms, equipment, supplies & vehicles utilized at the account, maintaining appropriate inventories and maintenance checklists.
- Sound judgment and decision-making skills, with a 'hands-on', problem-solving approach, ability to remain calm under pressure, and ability to take control of incidents.

District / Branch Manager

The Branch Manager is responsible for the business development, operations, and profitability of all physical security services within their assigned Security accounts. This position normally reports directly to a Regional or Vice President of their region. The manager manages the day-to-day administration and reporting functions as per the client contract and company policies. The manager is also responsible for daily operational communication with client representatives.

Some duties and responsibilities may include:

- Generate new business through partnership with the assigned Business Development Manager/Sales representative.
- Coach, counsel, and develop personnel to allow for their competency and growth.
- Work with all levels in the organization to identify, analyze, and solve problems and create opportunities for continuous improvement.
- Maintain the confidentiality of all information and data
- People management: Implement standard security operations at each client facility, and ensure compliance through regular site visits, review disciplinary actions for consistency and propriety
- Contract compliance; ensure that contract-required training and screening elements for security personnel have been met; quality assurance and contract compliance
- Oversee and manage administrative and operational functions, including payroll, billing, accounts receivable, scheduling, recruiting, training, etc., for the district
- Purchasing/asset management: request the necessary equipment to perform security functions
- Recruiting: coordinate with the Human Resource Shared Services team on recruiting efforts
- Setting and management of rosters: ensuring all shifts are filled with appropriate staff
- Training: Manage the training program of

Desirable skills and qualifications may include: college degree in business administration or equivalent experience; plus 5 years of business management experience, including supervisory, proven experience in security or a related field, prior security-related project management experience in a multi-location environment with demonstrated ability to deliver efficiencies, work history to include demonstrated ability to organize and manage the process required to maintain compliance for licensing and training functions, willingness to travel, demonstrated experience within a client service environments, demonstrated ability to build and maintain Client relationships, highly developed interpersonal skills, a commitment to the company values and policies, including equal employment opportunity, human rights and occupational health and safety principles and practices, commitment to continuous improvement and customer-focused quality service delivery, satisfactory results of a national police record background check upon delivery, satisfactory results of a national Police record background check upon employment and on an ongoing basis, Ability to work in a team-oriented management environment while having an entrepreneurial attitude.

all employees to ensure career paths are developed and a succession plan is in place
- Tender process for the retention of all contracts
- Performance/budget compliance: Responsibility for the oversight of Key Performance Indicators designed to meet contractual expectations, to include tracking cost savings initiatives
- Ensure all policy and procedures are followed, including pricing guidelines

Human Resource Manager

Human Resource personnel usually work out of District or Branch locations. A great deal of flexibility is required as they often travel to various sites around the country for potential overnight stays. Their work will be with the HR Operations Director for the business area.

The Human Resources position manages employee relations. They must have a strong knowledge of employment law and a proven talent acquisition record with solid employee relations skills.

Some duties and responsibilities may include:

- Work closely with operational management teams to develop line management capability and implement good people management practices.
- Lead and advise HRAs with managing ER cases, recruitment and selection, and remuneration issues.
- Support and encourage positive employee relations, engagement, and communication across all operational contracts.
- Build and maintain constructive working relationships with local/regional Trade Unions and employee representatives, and lead consultation at the operational level where required.
- Provide HR support for organizational change, new business, and restructuring activity, supporting HRAs and line managers where required with redundancy situations and working with the HR Shared Services Team as appropriate.

Desirable skills and qualifications may include: experience of operating in a complex, commercial and multi-divisional organization, detailed understanding of all aspects of HR management, Bachelor's degree in business or related field, 5+ years' experience, demonstrable track record of devising and implementing successful HR interventions with bottom line contribution, solid and up to date knowledge of practical HR principles and practices and employment legislation, good stakeholder management and communication skills at all levels, strong interpersonal skills, flexible with travel to various locations as the needs of the business dictates, good understanding of human capital measurement, ability to use word, excel, power point & outlook email & calendar.

- Work with the HR Operations Director and the HR Shared Services Team to ensure resources (ops and HR) are available to support mobilizations, to develop personnel, and ensure ownership of activities.
- Support management and HRAs with the local implementation of cultural change initiatives and embed organizational values and behaviors in existing and new business.
- Support the HR Operations Director in the implementation of succession plans, which help identify and develop high-performing people
- Maintain confidentiality of all information and data.
- Deliver core HR activities for the business, ensuring consistency and legal and company compliance, e.g., pay reviews, grievances, disciplinary, recruitment and selection, mobilization, and transition.
- Analyze HR data to identify trends and take action on the improvements needed.
- Identify mid to long-term training needs, priorities, and resources for other HR activities.
- Support the operational teams' responsibility to maintain H&S standards and ensure these are incorporated into HR practices.

Recruiter

The Recruiter position is responsible for recruiting, interviewing, and selecting qualified candidates. They work closely with the account manager to determine any specific requirements of candidates as needed.

Recruiters search for qualified professionals through many different sources, including referrals, job boards, Internet mining, and even networking events. A recruiter must build a large network of professionals and locate top talent in their field of expertise. This is the basis of their job.

When it comes to staffing, recruiters are the resource. This fast-paced profession requires extensive verbal and written communication as well as sales and negotiation skills.

Some duties and responsibilities may include:

- Source and recruit candidates through various means for hourly and exempt positions
- Know the client location, culture, job-related responsibilities, and physical requirements of each position.
- Create pre-screening questions to filter out unqualified candidates
- Source available talent databases, utilizing internal referrals, and connect with development community contacts for candidates
- Maintain compliance by reviewing requisitions, creating jobs, launching jobs, documenting the status of applicants, and closing jobs
- Interview qualified applicants to determine if they meet job requirements and quality standards
- Communicate with internal customers
- Communicate with AMs, DMs, and VPs the status of openings, facilitate the AM interview with a sense of urgency, follow up to understand why one is selected and another is not
- Select and process qualified candidates
- Ensure applications and pre-employment forms are completed
- Ensure all hires have passed the required background and drug tests
- Ensure completion of company/district requirements (fingerprinting, licensing, etc.)
- Periodic follow-up with new hires after 30 – 60 days

These positions comprise a small portion of the security industry - believe me, there are many more. With such a wide scope of service, every aspect of business will usually have some form of security.

Security is a large industry, and according to the IBIS World Industry Report on Security Services in the U.S., it is still expected to grow by over 6% in the upcoming year. So, the need for more positions will continue to rise.

Desirable skills and qualifications may include: staffing experience, minimum of 2 years recruiting experience, computer skills, flexible scheduling, ability to travel, knowledge of employment law, sales orientation, excellent people skills, phone skills, interviewing skills, results driven, professionalism, good judgment, organized and supports diversity.

Each position will have unique challenges and should be handled according to the job responsibilities. You will receive the necessary training for each position, but it will be up to you to be prepared. Some positions will require more customer service focus (such as a lobby desk officer), while others will require more security consciousness. Please know the difference. Regardless of the focus, *never compromise security for customer service.* It can and oftentimes will come back to haunt you. While every job requires the customer service aspect, always remember why you are there in the first place....SECURITY. Please keep this in mind when performing any job.

CHAPTER 7
WHAT EVERY SECURITY OFFICER NEED TO KNOW

Learning objectives

After reading this chapter, you should be able to

- Define what obligations you have to employers, and what you don't.

- Identify the differences between private security and public law-enforcement.

- Understand the importance of attendance.

- Balancing work and personal life.

- Define Standards of Professionalism.

- Identify tips to satisfying clients.

- Define the importance of being licensed.

- Identify what authorities Security Officer possess.

- Understand why unbilled overtime is frowned upon by employers.

- Define what steps to take if you feel you were wrongfully terminated.

Roy Wyatt

WHAT EVERY SECURITY OFFICER NEED TO KNOW

CHAPTER 7
WHAT EVERY SECURITY OFFICER NEEDS TO KNOW

Let's face it, Security Officers need information. The more informed they are, the better they are at performing jobs and making choices for themselves, enabling businesses to grow. But all information isn't found in books or written in policy and procedure manuals. Much of it is learned and comes by trial and error.

This section provides information that all Private Security Officers can find helpful in their personal and professional lives.

■ What Obligations They Have to Employers, and What They Don't.

Usually, once a security professional's shift ends, their day is over, and they go home. Very seldom are they required to stay over—maybe 30 minutes if someone is running late. Occasionally, you may get called to work on a day off, but it's your choice. You cannot be forced to work on your scheduled day off.

You show up on time, do your job, and when your relief comes in, you pack up and leave. Other than that, what obligations do you have to your employers? What about when your relief calls off, or there's a family emergency, and you must go home? Is it fair for your boss to get upset when you can't stay over or work on your off day? Do you owe them a good excuse for why you can't? Don't get confused! Or better yet, allow employers to determine your obligations.

You need to know what you owe your employer for that paycheck, and what you don't.

Five things you OWE to your employer.

Performing your absolute best every day!

You did your best at the interview and impressed the boss. Now, the real work begins. It's time to put your money where your mouth is. Based on your performance, your best is now a requirement. The employer is now counting on it. You are expected to perform at your best every day, not just some days.

This may sound harsh if you're bored, tired, not committed, or having a bad day; however, the job doesn't care. Clients and their customers are counting on you to perform at your best. You are expected to deal with issues and not allow them to affect your work performance. If you need to search for another job, do so off-duty. But don't slack off. This isn't fair to your employer, the client, its customers, co-workers, and yourself. As long as you work for the employer, you owe it to them to put your best foot forward, each and every day.

Your Creative Solutions

Work is a place to solve problems, bigger and thornier problems all the time. You learn something new and grow your flame a little more whenever you solve a problem at work.

> ### THINKABOUT IT
> Why is it important to be truthful to your employer?

Even though a job description might be boring, it's still in your best interest to bring your whole brain and heart to your role, as long as you have it, according to Liz Ryan, Influencer (Founder and CEO, Human Workplace; Author, "Reinvention Roadmap").

The Truth

Telling the truth is not always easy, but it's always right. Regardless of how it feels or affects someone else, your employer needs to know the truth about what happens at work and at the client's worksite.

Don't confuse work relationships with friendships. Oftentimes, these lines are blurred. Even though it may affect your relationship, telling the truth should not be an option. If you feel you cannot, you're too close. Don't risk losing your job over another employee.

On the other hand, how can a problem ever get fixed without you speaking up? If no one's listening and you're tired of your words falling on deaf ears, do something about it. Don't waste your time or energy on people who don't want to fix the problem. Find another employer that values your opinion and resolving issues.

Show you care

You don't have to care for anything when you're alone, but you do when working for someone else. You're not just being compensated for your work alone. All property, equipment, co-workers, and customers are also part of the package. Everything you use must be properly cared for.

When you take a job, it's your role. Take good care of everything you use and everyone you work with. You're always part of a team, even when working alone.

Integrity

Unfortunately, what's expected from most jobs doesn't always work out. It's too stressful, boring, you don't like your boss, and you're working too hard. None of which you expected. When you're not satisfied, it's easy to bash the job to family and friends – even co-workers. But what does complaining get you? Temporary relief at best, you still must return to work the next day.

Complaining about your employer isn't a solution to your problem. Furthermore, it tarnishes your brand as a person with integrity and kills your reputation. When you complain, the implicit message is that you're trying to rally support for your way of thinking. Not only is it bad for others' health and welfare to listen to you, but you'll find that colleagues will think twice before being linked to you.

If you want things to change in your career, you must make changes. But don't bash the job. After all, you interviewed and accepted the position, aware or not of its requirements. Move on and find something that better suits you.

Five Things You DON'T Owe Your Employer

Your Contacts

All businesses could use more customers. More customers mean more money to market and produce more products and services. And you guessed it – make more money! Without clients, security providers could not exist. They're constantly looking for avenues of increasing clientele, even to the extent of asking employees for their personal business contacts.

> Complaining about your employer isn't a solution to your problem. Furthermore, it tarnishes your brand as a person with integrity and kills your reputation.

Go ahead and provide them with sources of possible future contracts. If they have a referral program, with luck, you might get paid for it. However, it's not your job, and employers can't make you. It's unethical for employers to expect you to give up your personal contacts to further their gain, especially without compensation.

Your Health

The tragedy of the white-collar working world is that we pretend our bodies don't exist. Your brain can't function unless your body gets rest and exercise. It's not right for your employer to expect you to trash your health for the job. Speak up if you're not feeling well.

Don't let a weenie manager browbeat you into coming to work sick and infecting your co-workers, or worsening your own health. If they won't let you work from home when you're under the weather or take a sick day, get your resume up to date.

Your Personal Life

Everyone needs to learn the script we call "It's Impossible" to deal with managers who ask you what you've got scheduled at night or on the weekend that would keep you from working extra hours.
What you have planned in your personal life is nobody's business but yours. Here's the script:

BOSS: Joe, can you stay late tonight to get those invoices out?
YOU: Not tonight, but I can do them tomorrow.
BOSS: What's going on tonight?
YOU: Unmovable plans, but don't worry -- I'll do it tomorrow.
Don't start explaining that your kid has a hockey match or your wife's barbershop chorus has a dress rehearsal that you have to attend because you can't make the concert. The minute you open that vault, you can kiss your personal priorities goodbye. Learn to say "Wish I could! - but it's impossible" with a smile on your face.

Unearned Loyalty

Be wary of any employer that tells employees they should be loyal, just because they work there. Loyalty, like respect, is earned. You might be loyal to a boss who's always had your back, but that's different than being loyal to a corporation or an institution.

If you get a call from a headhunter about a job that sounds interesting, it's your right to call back and learn everything you can. You don't have to stay with a sinking ship and be the person who turns the lights out.
That's what "stay bonuses" are for.

It's appropriate and ethically correct to take care of your own and your family's interests before your employer's, and that's what anyone would do unless there is personal loyalty in place - loyalty that's been earned by past actions. Run away from people who tell you where they think your loyalties should lie.

Your Soul

Your job might include unpleasant aspects, like bureaucratic processes or boring meetings, but your job shouldn't require you to pretend to be someone you're not. If you wake up at night with your heart beating too fast because you can't stand the person your job requires you to be, get out!

You have one lifetime. You get to make your mark here on our planet, and that means you get to make choices, and you must. You don't have time or energy to waste with people who don't get you and value you the way you are right now, according to Liz Ryan Influencer (Founder and CEO, Human Workplace; Author, "Reinvention Roadmap)"

■ The Difference Between Private Security and Public Law Enforcement: Why Private Security is Often the Best Option for Providing Security.

The decision to have off-duty law enforcement or a private security firm is always difficult. Choosing State, County, or Municipal police will always have some unforeseen drawbacks. Here are some reasons why Security Officers is most often the best choice when needing security than public law enforcement.

1. Private security firms have more authority on private property than police; in addition, private security firms represent the property owners, while the police, even off duty on special assignment, represent the city, county, or state they work for. Police officers (even off duty) have to follow the guidelines outlined in the 4th and 14th Amendments of the US Constitution.

> Define what responsibilities you owe to your employer?

2. The police cannot stop anyone to ask if they live on the property, what they are doing, etc. This is a violation of a person's Constitutional Rights, which could open the police or property owner up to a civil suit. The police are not allowed to speak to anyone unless they have a reasonable suspicion that a crime may be afoot; further, they must be able to articulate this suspicion in clear language. Private security can interact with anyone at any time. Because they do not represent the Government, and the Constitution does not apply to private security.

3. Off-duty law Enforcement working a part-time job: Private security officers treat the job differently because it is their full-time employment. Private security officers also perform many tasks or duties that would be considered "beneath" most beat cops... Part-time employees are often not as dedicated as full-time employees.

4. **Legal ramifications of any issue on a part-time job.** The Law enforcement officers are less likely to get involved because of legal issues that might affect their

"full-time" law enforcement status. A civil suit or other legal issue could cause them to lose their full-time job.

5. Off-duty police are expensive. Two security officers cost almost the same as one off-duty policeman. This means more manpower keeping your property or venue safe for less money.

6. There are also civil law issues. Police work in the "criminal realm." They are not allowed to become involved in civil matters. Property owner rights, lease agreements, and other such issues are civil matters. The police have no knowledge or responsibility in these areas. Private security firms do. **Private security operates in both the civil and criminal realms.**

> **Difference between Private Security and Law Enforcement**
> The differences between public policing and private security: The public police are a government service provided at local, county, state, or federal levels. Public police follow strict requirements, training, and certification. ... Private security is a service provided by private companies.

7. Insurance Liability; will be insurance. Will the city, county or state agency cover any and all liabilities for an off duty police officer working on private property? Private security companies have Certificates of Insurance naming their clients as the Certificate Holders.

8. The US Supreme Court has ruled – **"it is not the duty of the police to protect the individual citizen**..." Warren v. District of Columbia, 444 A.2d 1 (D.C. App. 1981). Private security can and does protect all persons on the property of the client.

Police have a very difficult job. They are not specifically trained to protect private property. Properly qualified, equipped, and supervised security is always a better, more cost-effective option.

■ The Importance of Appearance

- How you look affects your confidence
- How you look determines attitude
- How you look affects performance
- How you look determines others' perceptions
- How you look determines how others relate and ultimately treat you

The appearance of a Security Officer is essential. They represent not only themselves but also their Clients and the Security Company they work for.

Upon hiring, officers will be issued a uniform. The specific style issued will depend on the account to which they are assigned.

Security officer uniforms are based primarily on a traditional police uniform, with the exception that traditionally, security firms have opted for more economical, less feature-packed selections. Because security companies have many uniform styles, they are very flexible in adjusting to clients' desired image.

An officer's uniform should project a presence while distinguishing the company he/she represents. It is their badge of honor and should be worn as such. It symbolizes who you are and what you stand for without ever saying a word to the world. It represents duty, honor, respect, a belief in a set of values, and professionalism. Not only will visitors gain an impression of the organization, but Employees in the facility will have more respect for the Security Officer and their organization.

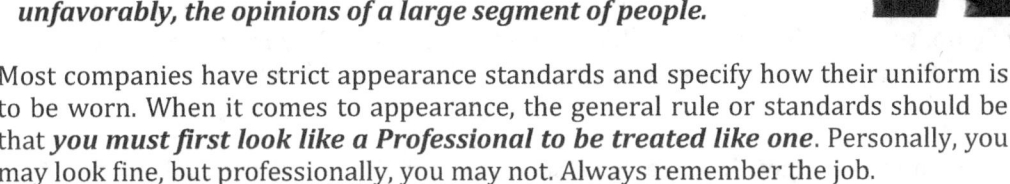

The primary duty of a Security officer is to deter criminal activity, and your uniform is a valuable tool in maintaining this effect.

> *Your presence can influence, either favorably or unfavorably, the opinions of a large segment of people.*

Most companies have strict appearance standards and specify how their uniform is to be worn. When it comes to appearance, the general rule or standards should be that *you must first look like a Professional to be treated like one*. Personally, you may look fine, but professionally, you may not. Always remember the job.

In my experience, most security officers do not read Company handbooks and end up asking questions that can be avoided. It is every employees responsibility to read, understand, and comply with their company policies. In most instances, Security officers will be required to sign-off confirming they read and comply with the policies being issued a company handbook.

As with any industry, you will find some officers who do not meet the company uniform and appearance standards. Do not be discouraged. As difficult as that may be, not too many things will go unnoticed. It may not appear that way at first, but usually, time will inevitably reveal the real consequences of all things.

> Define why appearance is so important?

If you see anyone out of uniform, kindly bring this to their attention. If you're uncomfortable, inform their Supervisor instead. However, if you decide to address the issue yourself, pull them aside away from others. It always helps to compliment the officer in other areas to let them know their work is valued and appreciated. Using tact, inform them of the policy and how their appearance affects the entire team's outlook. You never know –some officers respond better hearing it from a co-worker than a boss.

Uniform Issuance

Your employment status may often dictate the number of uniforms issued. Generally, full-time employees may be issued more because of their work schedule.

> In my experience most Security Officers do not read Company Handbooks and end up asking questions that can be avoided.

Do not be discouraged if you are not issued your full set of uniforms during start-up. To allow everyone to be outfitted, companies must balance the inventory on hand. What's not issued then will be ordered and provided at a later date. In some cases, only one set of uniforms is issued during orientation. Once officers start work, their manager of accounts will order their remainder.

Note: Uniforms should be returned back to the company if your employment ends.

Items on Uniform

To be consistent with the values and appearance standards, typically, no civilian attire should be worn with your uniform. If it's authorized, it will be very limited, such as a hat if the weather permits. Usually, rank, company training insignia pins, and badges will oftentimes be the only allowable items on the uniform. You may also be required to keep a pen and pad on hand as well. Please check your handbook.

Rank Structure

Like Military and Law Enforcement, security sometimes utilizes rank to designate leadership and responsibility. Some of the ranks you may find are corporal, Sergeant, Captain, Lieutenant, Major, and Colonel. As the rank goes up, so does the responsibility.

■ Can They Work for Multiple Security Companies?

There seems to be an unwritten rule of thumb among security companies that one officer cannot work for two different companies at the same time. This has everything to do with company loyalty.

Although this question has been posed many times, I have not seen any literature or company handbook stating you cannot. Although officers have often expressed that their prior Security Company would not allow this, still, no one has produced anything in writing. However, with all the security providers, I'm certain there may be some.

I know that any proprietary and confidential information employees obtain from one company cannot be disclosed to another, for obvious reasons. Security professionals have access to company information and intricate details of their processes and procedures. Certain information is vital to a company's success and reputation. If divulged, it can be harmful and provide an unfair advantage to competitors.

Because security professionals have such information, confidentiality clauses stating they will not disclose such information may be signed.

> **THINKABOUT IT**
> Why is it so important to keep company information confidential?

If working multiple companies is a concern, please consult with your Human Resources personnel or speak with the recruiter prior to being hired. This information may also be found in the Employee Handbook.

■ How to Balance Work and Professional Life.

All work can be stressful at times. As the pace of businesses increases, employees and managers are taking on additional responsibilities and are faced with delivering to ever-tighter deadlines, often with fewer staff. To manage these workloads, individuals are having to endure longer work hours, with feelings of stress and possible loss of control.

The pressures put on individuals' time by the organization then have a negative impact on individuals' personal lives, which in turn increases the feelings of stress and dissatisfaction, and creates a never-ending circle. 71% of respondents to The Management Agenda reported that they experienced stress due to work. When asked to define what they meant by stress, some of the key words used were anxiety, overload, loss of control, pressure, and long hours at work with insufficient time for personal activities. *One respondent summed up stress as "the feeling that you are working at your limit and that something is about to happen to cause the house of cards to collapse."*

To prevent this stage of exhaustion, it is essential to balance work and personal values in your life. Spending time with family and friends, exercising, maintaining hobbies, and engaging in religious or spiritual activity all serve as key factors in balancing work and life.

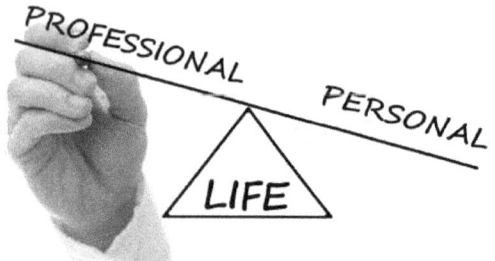

Time management is of the utmost importance. Employees must learn to control their workloads while not investing all their effort and time into one area of life over the other, but creating a balance. They must set limits and use administrative systems adequately to support their work and family lives.

According to a barometer published in 2016 by the National Union of Family Associations, two-thirds of employees believe their employer isn't sufficiently helping them with their work-life balance. The truth is, it isn't the employer's responsibility. It's the employee's responsibility first to diagnose and understand whether his/her work-life balance is well-balanced or unbalanced and then make the necessary adjustments to change or correct it.

Without knowing every employee's situation (i.e., their personal goals, values, hobbies, family life situations, etc.), it's unfair for businesses to take the blame. Even if they were, they would have to exercise one method to fit everyone. However, what balance is for one employee is seldom the same for another. Furthermore, individual life balances are likely to change over time.

This is up to individuals. Success is limited without employees' accepting responsibility and personal involvement in bringing about change.

■ Without An Acceptable Attendance Record, Nothing Else Matters

Regular attendance is an essential job function. Employees who repeatedly show up late and call off sap their morale, cost employers overtime expenses, and reduce employee engagement.

> Poor attendance saps the morale of employees, costs employers overtime expenses and reduces employee engagement. Poor attendance takes supervisory time and attention and often results in disciplinary action.

You are committed to working certain schedules and must report to work on time. Security cannot have any gaps in coverage. If you relieve another employee, they depend on you to be on time as well.

Poor attendance by employees becomes a burden on the company and the rest of the staff. Because of the drop in productivity their absence causes and the extra work handed to other staff members, which impacts morale, they are a financial burden to the organization.

Most companies understand that unexpected circumstances do happen. For this reason, a set of call-off procedures is generally in place to accommodate employees' tardiness or absences.

If you cannot be on time for any reason (i.e. overslept, vehicle broke down, medical emergency, etc.), it is your responsibility to notify your employer and explain the circumstances. In most cases this may be the on-duty Supervisor, Field Manager, Service Assurance Center, etc.

Security companies may also request documentation to substantiate your absence. So if you were sick, a doctor's note may be requested, but not required. If you are out of work for injury or illness for longer than 3 days, your company may require documentation to return to work. Please check the policy.

Disciplinary matrix

Employees who violate company attendance policies are disciplined under the company's progressive disciplinary matrix. If they receive enough absences/tardiness in a certain period of time, their employment may be terminated.

Officers who constantly make excuses for being late may as well stay home. This lack of respect for the profession, job, co-workers, clients, and customers will not be tolerated and will only lead to industry turnover. Poor attendance saps employees' morale, costs employers overtime expenses, and reduces employee engagement.

> The lack of balance between the personal and professional life can cause a burnout, a syndrome that includes emotional exhaustion, depersonalization of relationships, patients and the work, reduced sense of accomplishment (negative self-evaluation), and can be associated with impaired job performance and poor health.

■ Why most Security Contracts don't have Automatic Rate Increases

A common percentage of a 3% increase is a widely used amount that many companies pass on to their employees annually. This will vary significantly by company, as some may only be able to afford $0.50 cents or more/less. Now, this may not sound like much to the average officer, but depending on the number of company employees and various rates, this can be a substantial amount when looking at the total cost.

> Define why attendance is so important?

To authorize employee increases, companies have to forecast and maintain budgets and be supported by an increase in revenue. Because of this, annual increases may not be a guarantee, *nor is it usually built into* a majority of security contracts... especially the smaller ones. Except for some larger contracts, it would behoove the Security Company to re-negotiate rates after each year. Since bill rates come from clients, revenues will likely need to be increased to allow for an officer's raise to take effect, unless it's in the contract. So even though security officer wages are paid by the Security Company, the amount is largely based on Client bill rates.

The main reason security officers don't get automatic increases

Perhaps the biggest impact of receiving annual increases is the value clients place on jobs themselves. Clients determine bill rates, which in turn determine officer wages. Clients are very aware of the rates. With that said, they attach rates to what they believe the job security officers perform on their accounts. Unless they believe the jobs require a certain education, specialized training, skillset, or certification, chances are they won't be willing to adjust their rates regardless of how well they're performing.

> Unless clients believe the jobs require a certain education, specialized training, skillset, certification, and its importance, chances are they won't be willing to adjust their rates.

If employees are satisfied with their current wages, an annual increase may not be a problem. If they're not and looking for advancement opportunities with more pay, annual increases should be brought up during the interview process. It can easily be obtained if the Recruiter doesn't have this information on hand.

In Private Security, clients determine wage rates for contracted employees. Any change in this must be warranted and approved by the client. That does not mean Security Companies cannot pay officers without bill rates increasing; it's just very unlikely because of their markup (profit margin).

In my experience with clients, unless it's in the contract (which is very rare), in order to grant automatic increases, many factors are involved. However, the two biggest impacts will be an increase in overall revenue and the performance of security contractors. Regardless of how well a security firm performs, if it's not in the budget, wage increases won't happen. On the other hand, if the contractor's performance isn't up to standards, regardless of how well the company did, it still won't happen. So overall, while I agree that since inflation isn't going down, pay should not stay the same either. But remember, security is a contracted service. The client has already put a monetary value on the services based on the criticalness, level of importance, and qualifications needed.

To make a better argument, Security Companies would do better to re-negotiate rates each or every few years. Without this, Private Security increases are few and far between—except maybe on some larger contracts.

■ What is a Professional Security Officer ….. Really?

The terminology "professional" is anyone who works in a profession. In most cases, you are required to attain a certain level of knowledge followed by a pledge or a code of conduct. That's hardly the case as it relates to Security Officers.

Most states requirements are similar in that you must be at least18 years old with no felony convictions and attend "training" that involves sitting in a class for a few hours watching video, and then taking a simple test. Now there are some states that do have higher standards, but not all. The ones that do require higher standards and continued training for development will go a long way towards professionalizing the industry. However, the inconsistency makes it difficult to legislate professionalism in this industry as a whole.

As someone who has spent several years in the security industry; there are a lot of professional security officers out there. I can also tell you too, that as the client base increases, certain job complexities, standards and expectations, technology, perceptions, and diversity of people, more professionalism is constantly needed and being sought after.

Security officers are often the first point of contact for employees and visitors at a business. Therefore, Security officers must have excellent customer service skills. They are also responsible for ensuring that those employees and visitors are authorized. This means the officer must know the relevant policies and procedures of the client and be able to apply them to their access control duties. Access control duties also require officers to be aware of, and know how to apply, relevant state and local laws in areas such as trespass, public disturbance, and, if necessary, the use of force. Many officers have first responder duties, requiring training and certification in First Aid and CPR skills.

In addition, Security officers are often in a position that exposes them to confidential information, whether it's related to an incident occurring in the workplace or protecting a company's proprietary intellectual property. Further, these responsibilities require officers to adhere to ethical standards, either explicit or implied, since clients rely on their trust and integrity.

> PROFESSIONAL IS NOT A LABEL YOU GIVE YOURSELF – IT'S A DESCRIPTION YOU HOPE OTHERS WILL APPLY TO YOU.
> - David Maister
> *True Professionalism*

Therefore, professionalism in the security industry must come from within. Professionalism starts with attitude; your attitude stems from character. Since your attitude will reflect in every situation, we must start with that. Situations will always change, but you must remain professional in responding and handling the situation.

When complaining, most people usually say the person did not "act" professionally, referring to their behavior. So, remember that your "actions" will often influence the behavior, outlook, and perception of others while performing your job.

Professionalism is your ability to maneuver in a given situation that projects a favorable outlook while maintaining job integrity. It requires the essential attitude and skill set from knowledge and experiences that when coupled together provides an acceptable level of service.

Professionalism isn't what you do, but how you do it. Yes, training gives you the necessary skills to perform the job, but how you perform it determines professionalism.

Some organizations work to enhance the professionalism of Security officers. If you truly desire professional status, seek out these organizations and pursue training and development opportunities. Officers should also seek employment with security companies and departments that embrace professionalism. Yes, some officers reinforce the stereotype, but the growing complexity of Security officer duties and responsibilities is opening the way for a proper professional Security Officer.

> Professionalism isn't what you do but how you do it.

Security officers will be taught the standards required to perform their duties. If they're just starting their career as a security officer, chances are their skills will be put to use performing many responsibilities. The different posts, although challenging, will provide some practical knowledge and experience in certain positions. Although this is useful in developing your interpersonal and communication skills, sometimes it's not enough.

Professional Characteristics

I'm sure everyone has their definition of what makes up a professional officer, but several traits and qualities set this breed apart from the "mediocre or average officer". These behaviors and characteristics, when exercised, make you more professional. These professionals make up the industry of not only what it should be, but also where it needs to be.

As the client base increases, so does the demand for more professionalism. Take a look at the traits below. If you have them, you are well on your way. If not, try incorporating them into your thought process and work habits.

Professionals understand they must first follow before becoming a leader.

Everyone must start somewhere, and without prior experience, it's usually at entry level with the basic qualifications to pursue a job. Where you go from there will largely rely upon your ability to listen, follow directions, learn as you go along, and apply yourself. Following directions will not only give you the ability to understand how someone else feels if put in a similar situation, but also allow you to operate with an effective means of getting through it.

Following directions is a fundamental skill taught from an early age. While it may seem logical and even straightforward to follow directions—be they navigational directions, product-usage directions, or procedural or instructional directions—failure to follow directions can be a waste of time. Other times, though, failure to follow directions can be harmful (suspension, loss of job) or even fatal.

> "If you want to govern the people, You must place yourself below them. If you want to lead people, You must learn how to follow them."
>
> — *Lao Tzu, Tao Te Ching*

Become a great follower. Along with the skills of vision and leadership comes the skill of "ability to follow." What I mean by this is the ability to identify and follow the patterns of success within your organization. Follow in the footsteps of others who are "great leaders." Here is what one great mind says about this concept.

In "Reinventing Leadership", Warren Bennis wrote, "Good leaders should also be good followers. If you're coming up within an organization, you must be a good follower, or you're not going to get very far. Leaders and followers share certain characteristics such as listening, collaborating, and working out competitive issues with peers."

Professionals, upon seeing issues, own it and fix the problem, not leaving it for someone else.

THIN-SKINNED is to be sensitive, especially to criticism and slights. **Thin-skinned** people are quick to take offense.

Believe me when I say nothing bothers a Supervisor or Manager worse than seeing something wrong that could have been corrected beforehand. Unlike the average security officer, professionals understand the team concept. Regardless of who's at fault, the team is looked at as a whole, and anything that can be corrected should be.

Have you ever heard the saying, "You are only as good or strong as the weakest link?" The same is true with security. It's human nature. Attention is usually drawn to mistakes, blemishes, or anything unusual.

A single task can be performed one thousand times correctly. However, the one time it is performed incorrectly stands out—and that's what people will remember.

Keep in mind that you are part of a team, so whatever happens to one impacts everyone. The more initiative you take in correcting mistakes, the better everyone's outlook will be. If you cannot correct the problem, inform your Supervisor and/or bring it to someone's attention who can.

Professionals have thick think. They are not moved by everything that comes their way.

Have you ever met people who reacted to information the moment it was received? They can be in the best of moods and then suddenly change as a result of what was said. Obviously, I'm not speaking of anything personal that may have transpired and they're made aware of, but workplace chatter.

These people I'm speaking of take information head-on and immediately formulate a response or reaction. And oftentimes, the reaction gets blown out of proportion, or a decision is made without proper investigation. These people have "thin skin." Everything gets underneath their skin, and their logic of thinking is temporarily disrupted.

Politics has never been for the thin-skinned or the faint of heart, and if you enter the arena, you should expect to get roughed up. Moreover, Democracy in a nation of more than 300 million people is inherently difficult.

- *Barack Obama*

As Security Professionals, especially those in Supervision and Management, you must not be quick to react. You will be faced with various forms of communication and must always remain level-headed and focused. If it's derogatory, it often helps to look at the source. It could be from a biased point of view, so all things should be considered.

Professionals accept criticism and not get hostile when confronted with it.

Accepting criticism is a necessary tool, especially in developing behaviors in the workforce. If you receive criticism, this indicates that your performance expectation in a certain area has not been met. This should be looked at as a tool to bring this area of improvement up to par......nothing more.

Too often, having invested so much in their work, some could have trouble accepting that their work performance could be improved. Many may become angry if their work receives anything except praise.

Professionals use good judgment and common sense.

No matter where a Security officer is employed, good judgment and common sense should always be part of the job. In a department store, Security officers should position themselves in areas where they can observe suspected thieves without being noticed by them. Security Officers should make no exceptions for anyone entering or exiting without proper identification at a facility where security is needed. That said, it is unnecessary to be too strict sometimes, especially when you see the same person coming to work every day, and he has forgotten his identification card. It's also crucial for security officers to know when to get involved in a possible criminal situation and when to call the police.

As you can see, Security Officers must possess a range of qualities that are often given a diminished view by the public. However, by possessing them, you are certainly on your way to becoming a professional.

■ The Measure to Satisfy Clients.

When it comes to client satisfaction, there is no one-way-fit-all approach or measure. Different clients require different processes and procedures that must be customized to their location of service. As Security Providers, this is the epitome of client satisfaction.

Security Companies must be able to provide a customized plan in the form of Post Orders, SOPs, Job Instructions, etc., that is specifically designed to accomplish the client's needs. Checklists (if needed) can be created to ensure certain jobs get accomplished; however, that's on an individual, customized level.

Meeting all customer needs will begin with client satisfaction, but not entirely. The rest and most needed will be how security duties are performed. Anyone can be trained to perform various jobs, but how duties are performed creates professionalism. This will largely depend on several factors, such as the officer's skill set, education, training, customer service, and maturity, to name a few.

- Do not allow complacency to sit in
- Don't slouch while performing jobs
- Always be alert
- Be very customer service friendly at all times
- Be even-tempered when at work

The more ongoing training Security Providers give employees equates to better-trained and qualified professionals. In attracting clients, better training increases overall proficiency. With more education and training officers receive, this equates to better client satisfaction, resulting in long-term contracts for Security Providers.

■ Why Weapons Are Not Used On Most Sites.

When we discuss weapons for defense purposes, it's often different in terms of the private sector vs. the public. There's more involved in obtaining, but also what type best suits the position you're performing. In my opinion, you shouldn't bring a knife to a gun fight. But if you get close enough, that knife will serve just fine. However, it wouldn't be an appropriate defense mechanism if everyone else is packing six-shooters.

We all know most security is contracted, and having said that, it raises some likely questions clients think about regarding weapons, such as:

- Can they afford to pay Security Providers for armed officers?
- Do they believe weapons/certain weapons are necessary?
- Are they willing to risk the responsibility of having security with certain weapons?
- Do they want the image?
- What's the likelihood of actually using the weapon/equipment?
- What's the value of the service they provide?
- Etc. etc. etc.

> Define some factors that would influence a client's decision to have/not have security with weapons.

The bottom line is that it's a matter of risk vs. reward regarding weapons used on client sites. Clients willing to take the risk will go the extra mile to ensure security professionals have the necessary equipment to defend/deter illegal behavior. Those who don't will never agree to the appropriate defense weapons until an unfortunate situation happens.

Having said that, I don't think there's a *one-method-fit-all-approach* when providing security, as each job site will have various risks. But each site should have the appropriate defense mechanism to handle the risk.

Sometimes your best weapon is NO WEAPON. It forces you to utilize your communication skills.

▪ Why Many Contracts Seem Temporary.

This question has been posed to me many times, and for good reason. Many officers begin working on contracts to later find that the contracts have been lost to another security provider, the job went away, or was cancelled. Now the officer must be displaced, take a pay cut, or risk being out of a job. Not good. No employee gets a job just to be informed they're going to be out of a job real soon. I can certainly understand their concern.

All security providers have contract terms with clients; however, newly hired employees seldom know their expiration date or care to know. From the client's standpoint, there needs to be coverage regardless of how short or how long the contracts exist.

Upon hiring, Security officers do not know contract terms. They're often elated to have the job and less concerned about when contracts expire. Perhaps too much faith in the Security Company that these jobs will last also plays a factor.

Jobs are contracted
First, understand that all security contracts have terms. These terms can range from month to month, annually, and up to 3 – 5 years or longer. Generally, most security contracts expire annually. However, that has little bearing on when they expire since some clients remain with the same security provider for decades. Many contracts renew annually or month-to-month after a specific term has been met. Newly hired officers, including most seasoned officers, won't know this. Understanding contract terms is usually the responsibility of the Manager of the account, DM (District Manager), and above.

Just as employees decide to leave employers with very little warning, so can clients. They pull the strings and have the option to terminate contracts and/or seek another provider as necessary. Understand that contract termination usually begins and ends with the client, but usually with a 30 - 60 day warning.

Remember, security providers cannot survive without clients. As a result, they go to great lengths to retain clients. If security companies could, they'd gladly keep every contract forever. No business wants to lose customers.

Losing contracts should always be a concern. If you don't already know, speak with your account manager. They can answer any questions regarding contract stipulations, including terms. They can also inform you of the likelihood/or not of retaining services if/when the terms end.

So, if you're the victim of a lost contract, remember it's not at the request of the security provider but likely because of clients' dissatisfaction. Many contracts are lost due to mistakes, poor performance, and a lack of professionalism. For this reason, it's crucial to provide the best services possible while performing duties.

■ Why Security Officers Need To Be Licensed.

With the exception of nine states (Colorado, Idaho, Kansas, Kentucky, Mississippi, Missouri, Nebraska, South Dakota, and Wyoming), the majority of states have security officer license requirements or a certification system. These requirements must be met before a licensed Security guard/officer can legally work.

That doesn't mean you cannot work unlicensed. Many do. In fact, not every security officer working is licensed, and not every company requires licensing. The ones who are understand the significance of being licensed.

Generally, being licensed denotes a professional who has a broader range of duties, responsibilities, and exercises more independent judgment. Unlike the term "security guard" licensed security officers may involve a higher level of training to respond to emergencies, operate emergency equipment, monitor alarms, perform specialized training (including handcuffing and restraints), act as a liaison between agencies, perform CPR/first-aid, and entrusted with hundreds of millions of dollars' worth of assets for the company. That calls for a professional officer who can think and act like a professional. Being licensed connotes professionalism, and in the modern era, most security companies and clients want it.

> **THINKABOUT IT**
> What is the purpose of licensing?

■ The Importance of Supporting Your Company's Business Model and Strategy.

None of us always agrees with every company decision and policy, but as Security Officers, it's essential to support the direction your employer is taking. Simply because you don't always see their vision doesn't necessarily mean it's not working or heading in the wrong direction. The truth is, we rarely agree with every business decision companies make in the first place.

When supporting company strategies, it's important to remember two things.

1. **Give your company the benefit of the doubt.**
   Unless your company is new, chances are it understands its direction and has a strategy for getting there. Simply because you don't understand its business doesn't

mean it doesn't.

2. **Realize your perception impacts others' perception, without necessarily being true.**

   It may not be evident at first, but your views on the company will eventually be hard to hide with your constant interaction with coworkers. Pretty soon, it will creep into conversations without giving much thought. When it does, it will become difficult for co-workers to think positively towards you and the company. Just because you don't, doesn't mean others don't. Don't potentially spoil it for them.

   Whenever we don't support company strategies, it hinders our performance and that of the company as well. Companies depend on their employees to be all in. That means showing up and delivering on the promise to support and conduct business conducive to developing and growing the company's business. If you cannot do that, finding another job is better.

■ What to do if they feel they have been Wrongfully Terminated

A wrongful termination is any firing that is done in violation of federal, state, or local laws; the terms of an employment agreement; or for reasons that go against public policy. When employees feel they have been wrongfully terminated, several options are available to them.

1. Termination can be appealed by providing any mitigating circumstances within a set period of time to your Manager/District Manager. All evidence will be reviewed, and a decision will be made to either uphold the termination or override the decision.

   > Define wrongful termination?

2. File unemployment claim – if you win, you will be allowed to draw unemployment benefits until a job is found or time limit expires.

The second option is usually what's carried out as most officers rather contact an outside agency in an attempt to get paid while looking for additional employment.

HERE'S HOW IT WORKS – Security officers will call the Unemployment Office and file a claim citing wrongfully termination. Once their information has been taken, if the Unemployment Office determines employee has a case, the Security Company will be notified and additional information requested referencing the termination.

Upon retrieval, all evidence will be reviewed. If a favorable decision on behalf of the employee is reached, a hearing with both parties involved will be scheduled. This hearing can be over the phone or at a designated location - whichever best suits both parties.

After the hearing, if it's determined that the employee was indeed terminated without just cause, the Security Company will award and provide benefits to the terminated officer for a set period of time and/or until additional employment is found. The length of time benefits will be awarded is based on the employee's tenure with the company.

> Define the benefits to avoiding unemployment claims?

In some instances, if necessary and if wanted, the employee must be re-instated to their prior status before termination. If this action is taken, I would encourage employees to work at another location. This will give both a fresh start. If the termination is deemed just, no benefits will be awarded.

What companies are doing to avoid unemployment claims
These are becoming more and more common for employers, and a ton of effort is being taken to reduce them. The money paid out is staggering, and companies are now taking a more involved approach in their termination process.

In an effort to reduce unemployment claims, security companies are becoming creative and looking for avenues to not only maintain good employees but also ensure a termination is warranted. Some ways they are responding are:

1. Getting upper-level Management or Human Resources involved before administering terminations;
2. re-training, and
3. Transferring employees to other accounts if necessary.

These claims have required security companies to go to great lengths to ensure the process is fair and to retain employees as much as possible. As a result, security officers are sure to get a fair chance at pleading any case before being terminated. So, if a termination is given, it's most likely warranted as other avenues have been exhausted.

■ How to Report a Workplace Injury

Being safety conscious is always of utmost importance when performing any job. Security officers must continually remain focused because of the complexity of some duties and complacency. It is each employee's responsibility to be safe when performing duties.

Security companies are always concerned for officers' safety and well-being, and programs are usually available to remind them. Supervisors and Managers will continually enforce this mindset through safety meetings as well. In addition, a list of safety hazards associated with each job should be on site and made available to all officers.

For workplace injuries, employees will be provided Workers' Compensation, including medical care and/or wage replacement, as dictated by individual and state requirements. These can be astronomical, especially medical expenses. To this end, Safety Programs have become a widespread concern as companies must budget for this expense.

> Who is primarily responsible for workplace safety?

When injuries occur on-site, they should be reported immediately to a Supervisor or appropriate personnel. A first notice of Workers' Compensation Injury form must be filed, and ESIS must be notified within 24 hours following the Incident. Some company policies require these reports sooner.

Your Manager is responsible for ensuring workplace injuries are reported to ESIS. They should be reported immediately as they happen. After completion, a claim number will be given at the bottom of the form. This will be used to track Incidents if needed at a later date. Once a claim has been filed, funds will, in most cases, automatically be paid out by the employer.

There are some gray areas involving reporting certain incidents, especially if no medical attention is needed. Most companies will require all incidents reported, even near misses or hits. Some injuries may not be apparent at the moment, but officers may seek medical attention at a later date. Without a claim, this may limit the officer's ability to seek medical aid down the road. To avoid this, a record should be filed for all incidents.

Worker without safety equipment caught in the machine and seriously injured. Other worker is trying to help him.

Having said that, there are two classification of records filed with ESIS and the distinction must be made know upon notification. One is a *"claim"* and the other is *"record only"*. When ESIS is notified, it's automatically assumed that a claim exists in most cases unless you inform them.

A *"record only"* incident is filed when _no_ or _limited medical assistance_ is needed.

Filing an incident as *"record only"* allows the incident or near miss to be documented without filing a claim. If the officer later decides to seek medical assistance, this will already be on file, and a claim can be processed more expediently.

Be sure to know your company's policy on this, and remember that safety is everyone's responsibility. Be aware of the hazards associated with everything you do. Be careful.

■ What Authorities do Security Officers Possess

This is probably the most misinterpreted piece of security officer responsibilities. It is not uncommon for people to believe that security officers are like the police and have the same duties and responsibilities as public law enforcement officers. Once hired, they often receive a wake-up call, assuming they have certain authorities when they don't. These authorities need to be clearly defined.

Security officers generally have the following authority.

The Ability to Enforce Rules

Unlike police officers who are employed by their city or county, private security officers are generally employed by private parties (individuals, corporations, or institutions) to protect human lives and physical property. They are actually ordinary citizens, no more, no less. Their main duty is to enforce the rules, regulations, and procedures of the employer, provided it's not illegal. Although Police and security officers may enforce similar rules, it depends on the situation and certain protocols followed.

For example, a security officer in a bank can enforce rules such as "no unauthorized parking, loitering, loud noises, must show identification, no shirt, no shoes, no service." Other examples can include enforcing whether the bathroom is for employees or is open to customers as well. The list goes on and on.

Security officers cannot discriminate when enforcing rules. The rules must be applied consistently and fairly to everyone.

If any of these general property rules are broken, the security guard can ask the person to leave the premises. Reasonable force can be used, and if the person continues to resist the security guard's instructions, the police can be called, and a citizen's arrest can be made. The person can thus be arrested and charged with trespassing.

The Ability to Detain and Arrest

There is no legal obligation for Security professionals to make arrests. Their ability to detain and arrest is governed by the same laws as that for private citizens, commonly referred to as a *Citizen's arrest*.

Under very strict circumstances, a security officer can detain and arrest a person who has shoplifted, attempted robbery, felony, or other serious offenses. Unlike Police officers who can arrest someone with probable cause (they suspect the person has committed a felony, whether or not it occurred, or without actually seeing it); a security officer must have proof.

This means the felony must have been committed, witnessed, or at least attempted in the security officer's presence before a citizen's arrest can be made. To put into perspective, Security Officers can only arrest if under these conditions:

- A felony has occurred
- The police would not be able to respond in time
- Your site/post orders permit you to make an arrest

When detaining an individual, it also must be done in a reasonable fashion, and it usually depends on the circumstance. Generally, requesting identification and a pat-down will ensure the individual doesn't have any weapons. If the situation dictates, the individual can be handcuffed.

In making the citizen's arrest, the security guard must tell the person being arrested that he is being arrested, the reason for the arrest and the authority to make the arrest. **Does the security guard always have to go through this verbal list?** *Not if the person to be arrested is in the middle of the crime or the attempt to commit the crime or being pursued immediately after the crime. But once the criminal is caught and being restrained, he must be told what offense he is being arrested for, if he asks, according to Gray-duffy, LLP.*

The amount of force necessary to protect oneself or one's property. **Reasonable force** is a term associated with defending one's person or property from a violent attack, theft, or other type of unlawful aggression. It may be used as a defense in a criminal trial or to defend oneself in a suit alleging tortious conduct.

Once detained, the security officers have to alert the police immediately. If not, the person may be detained unlawfully. They must also inform the police of the offense and file a criminal complaint.

The Use of Reasonable Force

A security officer can never use excessive force, but only reasonable force is permitted. It is the amount of force necessary to use against another person that is appropriate to protect yourself in the situation. The severity of crime, the dire situation, and the risk of harm to the security officer and other individuals must be considered.

Excessive force (sometimes called police brutality) refers to situations where government officials, legally entitled to use force, exceed the minimum amount necessary to diffuse an incident or to protect themselves or others from harm. Some may include, but not limited to, choking, improper handcuffing, foul language, application of pain, discriminatory slurs, and verbal threats – just to name a few.

In an ideal situation, the security officer will be able to contact law enforcement, have them confront the person, and attempt to make an arrest. However, that is not often possible, meaning that a security guard may have to use force. The use of force, especially deadly force, should always be the last resort. A security guard should try to communicate verbally and explore other options before resorting to force, unless he or she has no choice.

The legal authority for a security officer will vary by state. So if you are a security officer or interested in becoming one, learn about the legal authorities you hold. Above all else, remember you are not a police officer, but a security officer. As a security officer, you do have some legal powers. They are meant to help you do your job.

Disclaimer: This article is necessarily general in nature and is not a substitute for legal advice. Your State, local jurisdiction, company policies, and procedures may vary. Always consult with your company policies and HR departments before taking any actions affecting their interest.

■ How Bosses Look at Security Officers Who Resist Change.

Change is the one constant element we all must contend with. Change is inevitable if any business, especially the competitive security industry, wants to compete and continually grow. IT MUST HAPPEN!

Many times, responding to change has more to do with how the change came about than the actual change itself. In general, many people, including yourself, probably cringe whenever change happens. After all, we are creatures of habit, and none of us probably takes change well.

However, the most significant impact on minimizing people's responses and making them more accepting of change is "Explaining why the change is happening." Not doing this silently lets them know you don't care how they feel. And since they're the ones pulling the workload, they should at least have the respect of knowing why they must now do something different.

There will always be people resisting change, but the majority won't if they know why, and even more susceptible if they participated. For the ones that still resist change, after being informed, well, that's a different story. How do you now deal with them? It's simple. If you didn't get the opportunity to explain the change "beforehand," it doesn't mean it's not going to happen because a few employees don't like or agree with it. If it's now an approved method of performance, it must be done. The officer(s) who violate this should be treated under the company disciplinary guidelines for misconduct – NO EXCEPTIONS!!

> One measure of how creative you are is how you respond to changes in your circumstances and environment. An appropriate degree of flexibility is an admirable quality of Great Leaders.

It's tough to contend with change, but we don't always get the opportunity to make rules as managers. However, we must adequately train and explain to our employees why. If we do this, I'm confident officers will be more acceptable. But for the few that don't, don't let their attitudes and misconduct spoil it for the entire team.

■ All Contracts Do Not Come With Benefits.

To most employees, benefits are just as important as wages themselves as they provide a security blanket of health coverage for employees and their families. However, benefits are usually reserved for full-time employees - but not always. Some companies allow for part-time officers to accumulate benefits, provided they accumulate an amount of annual hours.

Benefits are paid by the client, so depending on the contract, they may/may not be offered. They may be included in bill rates or billed separately to security providers. To be sure, consult with your Recruiter and/or account manager. For those accounts without benefits, no worries. Most security providers provide supplementary insurance with several plans. From there, employees may choose based on their needs.

■ How Disciplinary Counselling Should Be Perceived.

No one likes to receive any form of disciplinary action. In fact, the word alone puts a bad taste in most people's mouths. However, if performance dictates, corrective measures need to be taken.

> Define the purpose of workplace disciplinary?

Discipline in the workplace is how supervisory personnel correct inappropriate behavior and ensure adherence to established company rules. It is not designed to punish or embarrass an employee. However, oftentimes the notion of "disciplinary" automatically sets a negative tone before any counseling can begin.

This notion automatically dictates employees' perceptions and, ultimately, their mood. Since everyone's temperament, maturity, outlook, and experience are different, their moods will vary greatly.

A common misperception of signing a disciplinary counseling is an "admission of guilt". Nothing could be farther from the truth. In the companies I've worked for and known, signing means "*only that it has been properly administered*" to you. There is an annotation on most forms for an opinion of agreement or disagreement.

If you are disciplined, your perception of the actions will impact your ability to overcome and move forward. I have witnessed officers who could not get over being disciplined and ultimately had to be terminated for lack of performance. Others took it in stride, and performance improved greatly. Those who did went on to become better officers, and some are now in leadership positions.

Regardless of the reason, remember that counseling is only for informational purposes and should not be taken personally. It's there to correct a behavior or violation of a policy or procedure.

Stages of Disciplinary
Companies utilize stages of disciplinary action to give officers chances of correcting performance, such as verbal warning, first written warning, final written warning, suspension, and termination. This informs employees of where they are being terminated if their inappropriate performance or behavior continues.

Not all offenses will warrant starting at the beginning as some will constitute more serious action. For instance, using abusive or offensive language will constitute a higher disciplinary than being 15 minutes late for work. Some actions will warrant termination on the first offense. Keep this in mind.

If you are in the disciplinary process, speak with your Supervisor and/or Manager. Consult with them on ways to improve your performance or behavior. This shows them you understand and truly want to better yourself. Believe me, most leaders don't like administering discipline any more than the officer receiving it. However, leaders must correct inappropriate behavior and put any personal feelings aside. *So, being upset or showing attitude toward your leader(s) after a disciplinary action isn't warranted and usually makes matters worse.* You must recognize and be able to perform at the level consistent with the job requirements, and attitude is a significant factor.

Take it from someone who knows. We rarely notice our own performance. Sometimes, we may need to be disciplined. Discipline is only there to help.

■ Why Bosses Don't Like Paying Overtime.

Many people like getting overtime pay. They don't mind working unscheduled time off to cover a post and, in return, receiving time and half pay. It's a win-win situation for both the officer and the Supervisor, right? Wrong.

That seems correct to the officer working the extra hours. To the manager in charge of the account, not so much. To them, it's a two-edged sword. On one hand, he/she is glad someone volunteered to work the extra hours, but on the other hand, he/she knows how the company looks at paying overtime.

Paying too much overtime will continue to be a major concern (for many security providers) and a topic of discussion in most managerial meetings. When overtime is paid out, the bottom line is that it means less money for security providers. If not managed properly, companies can easily begin paying out more than the client pays for services.

Why don't companies like paying overtime

Paying unbilled overtime raises a red flag to security providers, and for good reason. Whenever overtime is paid but Clients are not billed at the overtime rate, it usually indicates several things that companies look for.

> Paying overtime wages hurts company's bottom line. Besides that, it's an indication of other performance issues.

- ■ *Staffing issues*—Security is a contracted service, so all posts should have a designated officer to work specific days/hours. This can indicate that not enough manpower is on hand, and the account is experiencing staffing issues.

- ■ *Officers are overworked*. Overworked employees lead to fatigue. When fatigue sets in, mistakes begin to happen. If enough mistakes happen, this could jeopardize the contract and put everyone's job at risk.

- ■ *Companies are losing money by paying more for services than what's coming in*. Imagine you paying Officer Johnny $12.00 an hour, and your services being paid by the Client is $15.00 an hour. Officer Johnny has worked over 40 hours and now you must pay him $18.00 dollars an hour. For every hour Johnny works past 40 hours, the company is losing $3.00 an hour. What if numerous officers were in overtime? No company can afford to stay in business doing that.

Other areas impacted by overtime include: staffing, time off/vacation requests, call-offs, absences/tardiness, and training. These areas will be directly affected by overtime and must be controlled by whoever manages the account.

Managing overtime is such a critical component that if it consistently exceeds the company's allowable limit, managers can be relieved.

> **THINKABOUT IT**
> Why don't companies like paying overtime?

Billable overtime
Some overtime hours can be billable. This means Clients will pay officers at the overtime rate. Which types, if any, will always be in the security contract or agreement? Some approved overtime can be:

- ***Additional coverage request*** – At times, Clients may request additional coverage. Clients sometimes will pay overtime if this request is given within a certain period of time, usually within 24 to 72 hours. They understand the difficulty in requesting additional coverage in such a short period of time.

- ***CPR/First-aid Training*** – If this is a required contractual obligation, some clients may pay for this.

- ***On-the-job training (OJT)—This is the agreed-upon amount of time new hires*** will train to learn the job/position. Depending on the difficulty and critical nature, this can be anywhere from 8 to 40 hours. Very seldom have I seen Clients pay for more than 40 hours.

Overtime is a major concern, and security officers need to understand the complexity of managing. Although unaware, there's usually a good reason behind keeping overtime at a minimum.

Bottom line: Companies are in business to provide a service. In doing so, they expect to be compensated. If too much unbilled overtime is paid out, this defeats the purpose. Managers are known to be relieved from duty if overtime is not kept under control. So at the end of the day, it's not that bosses don't like giving overtime. They'd rather not jeopardize their job by doing so.

SUMMARY

- Security Officers owe their employer the following: Performing their best every day, creative solutions, the truth, showing they care, and integrity. They do not owe their contacts, their health, their personal life, unearned loyalty, and their soul.

- The **primary duty** of a Security Officer is deterrent, and your uniform is the most valuable tool in maintaining this effect. Besides that, their presence can influence either favorably or unfavorably the opinions of a large segment of people.

- To prevent exhaustion, it is essential to balance work and personal values in one's life. Spending time with family and friends, exercising, maintaining hobbies, and engaging in religious or spiritual activity all serve as key factors in balancing work and life.

- **Poor attendance** saps employees' morale, costs employers overtime expenses, and reduces employee engagement.

- The biggest impact on **receiving annual increases** is the value clients place on jobs themselves. Unless they believe the jobs require a certain education, specialized training, skillset, or certification, chances are they won't be willing to adjust their rates regardless of their performance.

- **Professionalis**m comes from within. It has nothing to do with your job, pay, or status. Professionalism isn't what you do but how you do it. Some characteristics of professionalism include:

  - Understand they must first follow before becoming a leader
  - Once they see issues, they own them and fix them. They don't leave it to someone else.
  - Professionals have thick skin. They are not moved by everything that comes their way.
  - Professionals accept criticism and do not get hostile when confronted with it.
  - Professionals use good judgment and common sense.

- To **satisfy the client**, five things must be done.

Roy Wyatt

1. Do not allow complacency to sit in
2. Don't slouch while performing jobs
3. Be always alert
4. Be customer service friendly at all times
5. Be even-tempered when at work

- Before **weapons are used** on client sites, they always determine the risk vs. reward.

- Generally, a **licensed Security Officer** denotes a professional who has a wider range of duties and responsibilities and exercises more independent judgment.

- Security Officers can always file an **unemployment claim** if they feel they were wrongfully terminated.

- Security officers have the **following authority**:

  - The ability to enforce rules
  - The ability to detain and arrest under the following circumstances
      - ☞ A felony has occurred
      - ☞ The police would not be able to respond in time, and
      - ☞ Your site/post orders permit you to make an arrest
  - The use of reasonable force

- All **Security contracts** do not come with benefits. Clients pay benefits, so they may/may not be offered.

- Paying **unbilled overtime** is an indication of three things to security providers:

  - staffing issues
  - Officers overworked
  - Companies are losing money

CHAPTER 8
GETTING TO THE NEXT LEVEL

GETTING TO THE NEXT LEVEL

CHAPTER 8
GETTING TO THE NEXT LEVEL

As with any profession, getting ahead requires you to be proficient at your current position, especially if promoting from within. However, certain qualities are more desirable than others that can tip the scale in your favor.

Leaders possess certain inevitable qualities that employers look for, primarily in keeping with their traditions and fostering a long-term relationship. Every employee represents their company, and employers are always looking to keep the sharpest knife in the pack.

Great qualities accompany great people. Let's look at the attributes employers look for that can get you to that next level.

■ Having a Winning Attitude

Everyone has bad days at times, and security officers are no exception. However, Security professional duties, if performed correctly, are looked up to—especially during difficult times. Security positions come with authority, governed by policies and procedures, coupled with maintaining composure and delivering on the promise of assisting in the situation with a commendable attitude. Every customer expects this attitude from security professionals.

Your "attitude" to me is more important than circumstances, successes, or failures. It is how I want to approach to world, and in return, how I want to be approached. A winning attitude is not about what other people think or say.

It's true that appearance, demeanor, and skills determine others' perceptions, but attitude always carries more weight as it is the direct communication with customers. We have a choice each day in how we embrace the world. Do we choose success or settle for the norm or "status quo"?

You cannot change the past or how other people will act. But the one thing you can control is your attitude, so you must start there. I can only wish that you find these words as motivational as I do in using the one thing I know I have, and that is a positive attitude. Regardless of profession, it is a major part of being successful in life.

A person needs to have a winning attitude in order to be successful in life. Below are seven suggestions that could help you develop a winning attitude.

1. Choose to be Positive - Develop the habits of thinking, talking, and acting positively. We all have the choice of how we will handle the daily situations we confront. It's very simple. Are you going to be positive or negative? Charles Swindoll stated it best in one of his quotes: "I am convinced that life is 10% what happens to me and 90% how I react to it." So if you respond to what happens to you in life in a positive manner, that is the first step to being a winner.

2. Passion—A desire and energy are needed as fuel to reach one's true potential. No amount of knowledge or skills will ever do without the driving force to put them to use. You should have a driving force deep within you to be successful.

3. **Belief** - You should be able to believe in yourself that you can do it.. You must believe you will win before you even attempt it.

> Attitude is more important than circumstances, successes or failures.

4. Think positively - I personally think that most of us try to win in life with the wrong mindset and attitude. We must think positively and get rid of the "negative thinking. We must learn to stay focused on positive thoughts and know in our hearts and minds that we are equipped with the right talents and gifts, that we can achieve anything we put our minds to.

5.   Strategy - This is your game plan. You should design a proper and realistic strategy to achieve your success. Remember, no plan is a plan for failure.

6.   Commitment - When you decide to take on a project or participate in anything in life, you must be committed. Your commitment to anything first starts in the planning and preparation – mentally, physically, and emotionally. You must be committed to everything it requires to accomplish your objective. Only after that can you be prepared to give the 110% it deserves. You should stay positive and never think about quitting. That is where true success is found.

> **THINKABOUT IT**
> Why is it so important to have a great attitude?

7.   Must have Value—Everything we do in life has a value attached to it, and oftentimes, we do not know it. The more value we attach to something, the greater our joy or pleasure. It will also determine our desire and what we're willing to sacrifice to achieve it. Without a clear system of values for yourself, believing in something with a passion that has no value to us is impossible.

A positive mental attitude is an absolute prerequisite for success. This attitude determines how well you do and how far you go in life.

ADVANTAGES OF HAVING A GREAT ATTITUTDE

Creates a positive environment

Helps to Achieve Goals and Career success

Stress reduction and management

Better health

Less sick days

Increases productivity levels

Produces more energy

Improves customer relations

■ Look the Part

Without a doubt, any job or profession will require you to look like you belong. In today's workforce, appearance is just as important as your skillset and experience. Without your appearance up to standards, you're likely to never get that second interview and passed over for promotions.

How you put yourself together tells employers more about you without a word ever being uttered. In fact, I have turned many away from interviewing upon seeing their appearance.

Most security jobs require Security Officers to wear a uniform. If your uniform looks like it was just removed from the dryer, you may as well go home. No one will ever take you seriously, and you would be an embarrassment to the company. Before you say a word, you have already set a course for future perceptions and judgments. For this reason, companies must adhere to strict uniform and appearance standards.

Some regulations can be vague and often leave room for interpretation, but nevertheless, this does not excuse an officer's appearance.

I have seen officers with multi-colored hair, inappropriate and excessive jewelry, and a too-large or too-small uniform that doesn't fit the security model, and quite frankly, I wonder if they are in uniform.

Security officers should, at a minimum, adhere to the following uniform and appearance standards:

- Men: clean/neatly trimmed facial hair
- Women: none or conservative makeup
- Women: no flamboyant hair styles/color
- Uniform, neat, and fit (unwrinkled, not too tight/loose)
- Trousers not hanging below the soles of shoes
- Footwear clean and/or polished
- Minimum or no jewelry
- Wear only authorized gear with a uniform

Security officers who look professional act and feel good about themselves. In return, others perception towards them will reflect a more positive approach.

■ Be Flexible

Today more than ever, we are challenged to be flexible -- in our work, our relationships, and in every other important aspect of our lives. However, due to our own fear, arrogance, resistance, stress, and obsession with being right, we often end up being inflexible to our own detriment and to the frustration of those around us (or so I've been told).

Being flexible is not about being weak, wimpy, or passive. Flexibility is a conscious choice, a powerful skill, and a valuable approach to our ever-changing, always-evolving world. We can be firm in our convictions, passionate about our beliefs, and clear about our intentions while being flexible enough to make significant changes and be open to new ideas along the way.

It is an advantage if you have the desire to succeed at anything you do. You will experience day-to-day difficulties. Delays and frustrations will also affect your demanding work and life when dealing with people. Sometimes you have to deal with situations that do not fit in or interrupt your schedule.

One measure of how creative you are is how you respond to changes in your circumstances and environment. An appropriate degree of flexibility is an admirable quality of Great Leaders. Being flexible means being responsive to change or adaptable to new ideas or conditions. It does not

Define some advantages of being flexible?

mean changing your mind, direction, or plans daily or second-guessing each strategy or action taken. However, the world around us is changing faster than ever, and Leaders will take advantage of the opportunities presented by this change.

Some areas where Security officers need to be flexible may include:

- holding over if someone calls off,
- following a procedure you may disagree with,
- wait for that job promotion,
- work on a scheduled day off,
- perform an unexpected job or task,
- change of work assignment
- work with someone you may not want to

An appropriate degree of flexibility is an admirable quality of Great Leaders. Being flexible means being responsive to change or being adaptable to new ideas or conditions.

No one can control every situation. Sooner or later, an unexpected event or decision will cause you to shift gears – sometimes unexpectedly. When it does, it's usually beyond anyone's control. Being flexible is necessary, not only in jobs, but also in life.

Most changes usually come from Clients, not the security provider, Supervisor, or Manager. Sometimes, they can be last-minute and require little time to complete. Always keep that in mind.

Employees who practice an appropriate degree of flexibility can be very consistent, while being bendable to a point that does not cause injury. You will face challenges in life and on the job, and those who are flexible are usually more creative in solving them. Practicing flexibility can be a powerful tool in the arsenal of a Great Leader. The bottom line is that if you do not bend, you will ultimately break.

Here are some tips on how being flexible can improve your life at work and at home.

1. It saves you time and energy
While some Security Officers are getting stressed out over last-minute changes, your ability to be flexible will have you checking your schedule to see where you can make changes. When officers are flexible, the reason for the changes doesn't really matter; they just deal with it and move on.

2. You expect change, even embrace it
Instead of Security officers being stuck with a rigid schedule, they will be better able to anticipate changes before they even happen. Develop the habit of asking yourself, "What changes could come my way today?" and you'll be less liable to stress out when they actually show up.

3. It allows you to move forward with less stress
When Security Officers are flexible, it's much easier to switch gears and move from one task to the next with little stress. Where an inflexible Officer might get stressed out at leaving one task undone because they were asked to help with a last-minute project, your newfound flexibility will allow you to jump into the new project easily, and just as easily return to your own work when the crisis has passed.

4. You get a reputation for being easy to work with when you're flexible.
If a Security Officer is flexible, they will get a reputation for being the person everyone wants on their team. There are only a few things that build a positive reputation better than showing people you are adaptable when the situation warrants it.

5. You present a much more positive attitude.
Unless you're a recluse, most Security officers will have to deal with other customers (internal and external) while performing their jobs. Officers must recognize that change is probable, especially when dealing with multiple customers, and being able to deal with it is a wonderful trait to have. Being flexible shapes that skill. People appreciate it when you are able to handle a change in situation without getting stressed and bent out of shape.

6. It shows you know how to "go with the flow.
John Crowe once said, "It takes a strong fish to swim against the current, even a dead one can float with it

Sometimes, standing up for what you believe in and going against the current is the right thing to do. There are also times when being flexible and going with the flow is more appropriate.

For example, if your job is on the line, or you're working with a team, you might want to show you can be flexible and do what your boss or team wants, whether it's what you want to do or not. Being willing to do what was asked of you will make an impact, whether it's relayed to you or not.

> *Tom Robbins once said, "Stay committed to your decisions, but stay flexible in your approach."*

7. It cures you of perfection

Some Security officers are perfectionists. Everything must be done or performed in a certain manner or standard. Many people's stress is directly attributed to everything having to be just so, and when the smallest things don't go as planned, they get freaked out.

Officers must learn to be flexible by letting go of the things they can't change. The thing is - there will ALWAYS be things you can't change. So being willing to accept that things are what they are will allow you to live a longer and happier life.

8. You are much calmer

Some Officers get freaked out by every little thing that happens. Learning to be flexible allows you to stay calm and deal with situations as they happen. If you do this, you'll have a positive mindset, feel more confident in your ability to handle the situation or crisis, and have a better outcome.

The point I'm trying to make here is that going with the flow doesn't always mean you're going against your ideas. It may be a matter of survival. You will sometimes have to endure a job or task in order to achieve your ultimate goal. Rise above the situation and do what's needed.

Here are some key elements to expanding your own capacity for flexibility in your life, which will lead you to greater peace, joy, and fulfillment.

1: Accept the change

Normally, when we're required to be flexible, it's because something has changed that we didn't plan for. Accepting the change, whether it's good or bad, is the first step towards remaining flexible.

2: Be willing to be wrong

Most of us love to be right and will do and say just about anything to avoid being wrong. Our obsession with this often gets in the way of going for what we want, saying what's on our mind, and letting go of our ideas of how things are supposed to be. When you're willing to be wrong (not necessarily or intended to be wrong), we free ourselves up and give ourselves permission to take risks, try new things, and approach things differently with a creative, innovative, and flexible perspective.

3: Get support and Feedback from others
The support and feedback of others are invaluable in so many aspects of our lives and growth, especially as they relate to our being more flexible. When we're going through changes in life or at work, we need support. The better we access support, the better we'll be at remaining flexible.

4: Don't take yourself too seriously
Taking ourselves too seriously creates unnecessary stress, pressure, and worry. When we're able to laugh at ourselves, this keeps things in perspective, and remember that most of what we deal with daily in life is not life or death -- we can take ourselves less seriously and thus have a more balanced, peaceful, and creative way of relating to things. There is humor in all of life – the good, the bad, and the ugly. It makes a lot of difference.

5: Know that it will pass
Tough times and stressful times happen, but they do not last forever. Realize the change you are going through is just a season and will pass.

6: Let go of attachments
Whenever we get attached to something – a specific outcome, a particular way of doing things, a rigid opinion or specific outcome, etc., we are by definition inflexible. Letting go of our attachment to something doesn't mean we negate our desires or intention, it simply means we let go of controlling every aspect of it, forcing the action, and our fixation on it being exactly the way we think it should be.

7: Maintain perspective
Maintain a positive perspective no matter what the situation. There's always something good that can come out of every change – be willing to look for it.

Many people find being flexible difficult. However, just as with our physical bodies, the more attention we place on expanding our flexibility, the more likely we are to do it. As we enhance our ability to be flexible, our lives can and will expand exponentially.

Article Source: http://mike-robbins.com/be-flexible/

■ Stop Making Excuses

Most of us are guilty of having done something we shouldn't have or of not doing something we should have. When we are questioned about our misconduct, do we accept responsibility and admit we are at fault? Usually, not. Instead, we make excuses.

Making excuses for mistakes is not new. In fact, we can trace this undesirable habit back to the Garden of Eden. For when God asked Adam if he had eaten of the tree he was commanded not to, Adam created the world's first excuse, "The woman whom thou gavest to be with me, she gave me of the tree, and I did eat." (Genesis 3:12) And when God asked Eve what she had done, she gave the world's second excuse, "The serpent beguiled me, and I did eat." (Genesis 3:13)

Excuses negate responsibility, and it is responsibility that separates man from the rest of the animal kingdom. Unlike other animals, we are responsible not for what we have, but for what we could have; not for what we are, but for what we could become. If we are to take credit for our successes, we must assume responsibility for our failures. Trying to hide our failures with excuses is like concealing a small hole in our garment with a large patch; it only makes the matter worse. This analogy is taken from Shakespeare, who wrote:

> He that is good for making excuses is seldom good for anything else
>
> –   Benjamin Franklin

"And oftentimes, excusing of a fault,
Doth make a fault the worse by the excuse;
As patches set upon a little breach,
Discredit more in hiding of the fault,
Than did the fault before it was so patch'd."

How to stop making excuses and start building a life

Excuses are harmful because they prevent one from succeeding. When we make excuses and repeat them often enough, they become a belief. The belief then becomes a self-fulfilling prophecy. For example, a sales rep discouraged by his poor sales starts to blame the price of his product. "No one wants to buy it because it's too expensive." he says. After repeatedly making this excuse, he begins to believe it is true. The result? Dismal sales. Compare this with a responsible sales rep. After hearing many prospects complain about the high price, he accepts responsibility. "It is my fault they are complaining," the rep says, "for I haven't justified the cost of my product by adequately pointing out its value." Once we accept responsibility, we can evaluate our actions and take corrective measures to find solutions to our problems. Excuses, on the other hand, are like stop signs; they halt our progress.

By refusing to make excuses and embracing responsibility, we reap many rewards. The successes brought by this attitude act as a foundation of self-respect, pride, and confidence. Responsibility breeds competence and power. By living up to our promises and obligations, we win the trust of others. Once we are seen as trustworthy, people will willingly work with us, for our mutual gain. So, making excuses can put the brakes on our progress, while accepting responsibility can lead us to the top.

1. **Realize that your success or failure depends on you.**
   It depends on your choices and attitude. Resolve to start accepting responsibility today. Don't find an excuse; find a way. Don't make excuses; make good. Remember what Winston Churchill said: " Responsibility is the price of greatness."

2. **Beware of rationalization**

   When you accept responsibility for your life and, learn to focus on the things which you can control, you will find it very easy to avoid making excuses when things go wrong. You must always accept responsibility for the things you do and the things you fail to do.

   We make excuses to hide behavior we are ashamed of. Rationalization is the process of trying to hide shameful conduct from ourselves. This is dangerous because we become unaware of what we are doing. However, you can fight rationalization by looking for cues. It depends on the choices you make. It depends because we become unaware of what we are doing. However, you can fight rationalization by looking for cues. It depends on the choices you make. It depends on your attitude. Resolve to start accepting responsibility today. Don't find an excuse, find a way. Don't make excuses, make good. Remember what Winston Churchill said, "Responsibility is the price of greatness." For instance, if someone challenges your conduct and you become angry, it probably suggests you are guilty as charged. Why would you get angry if you're innocent?

3. **From time to time, stop and examine your progress.**
   Compare where you are now with where you would like to be. Ask yourself why there is a gap between these two points. Don't make excuses. Make plans and take corrective action.

4. **When you make a mistake, accept responsibility;**
   Learn from it, and don't repeat it. Use your time to discover solutions instead of inventing excuses.

   People rationalize for various reasons. Rationalization may differentiate the original deterministic explanation of the behavior or feeling. Sometimes rationalization occurs when we think we know ourselves better than we do. It is also an informal fallacy of reasoning. What is holding you back from achieving your dreams? Is it a hard pill to swallow to think that YOU are the only thing between you and your dreams? "Don't complain, Don't Explain," Wayne Dyer.

Besides your Creator, Source, God, whatever title you are comfortable with, YOU are the only one you ultimately answer to. Therefore, YOU are the one who determines your destiny. To achieve it, you first have to dream it. You must have a burning desire for your dreams. Do you live your life making excuses for why you cannot achieve your dreams? Take a moment and think about what your excuses are. Are you fearful of failing? Are you harboring any of the 9 Negative Emotions?

1. Fear
2. Jealousy
3. Hatred
4. Revenge
5. Greed
6. Superstition
7. Anger
8. Lack
9. Victim Mentality

Living your life with these emotions assures you that you will live your life making excuses and never achieving your dreams. If you are using these negative emotions as excuses, they will make you a bitter person, holding dreams that are never fulfilled inside. How do you rid yourself of making excuses? "Our most important problems cannot be solved, they must be outgrown." Carl Jung.

Who is responsible for the way you think? YOU are responsible for your thoughts and beliefs. Therefore, you are in control. If you blame others for not achieving your dreams, get THEM fixed and see if that fixes YOU. Nope, you are 100% responsible, not something or someone outside of yourself.

What is the payoff for making excuses? Is it easier to make an excuse than to take responsibility? Maybe you are using these excuses to believe you are always right, to manipulate people, to purposely keep yourself from succeeding out of fear of success. There is always a payoff for our actions. That is why we repeat them. What's yours? What would your life look like if you couldn't use these excuses? Would you feel truly free? When you begin to realize that, why wouldn't you choose to eliminate excuses? Go into your imagination and dream about the life you would create for yourself if you could have anything you wanted. After you have captured that thought completely, how does it feel? Stay with the feeling. You can call on that feeling whenever you begin to make excuses about why you cannot do something, to pull yourself back to the reality you wish to create.

Can you create a rational reason to change? It has to be doable and it has to make sense. By not allowing yourself to make excuses, you open a Pandora's Box of reasons to change. Which will you select? When you make a choice, or if you choose all the options, you have just allowed yourself to manifest your dreams. How do you continuously reinforce this new way of thinking? Talking to your subconscious. Your conscious mind is dumb as a rock. It only regurgitates back to you what you have memorized. Your subconscious is the smart one and that is what guides your every thought. Therefore, wouldn't it make sense to tap into your subconscious and change what you don't want?

Change all those thoughts and feelings that just seem to pop up out of nowhere and are not constructive. You must do things that make you at peace in order to tap into your subconscious. Before you go to sleep each night review your positive affirmations instead of reviewing what went wrong during the day, or conjure up one of the 9 negative emotions. By implanting positives into your subconscious at night, you'll have 8 or so hours to recycle those thoughts through your subconscious so that during the day, your subconscious will return only positives. Making excuses instead of creating dreams is self-destructive. Excuses keep us stuck. Breaking lose from excuses free us to reach our dreams and become the people we wish to be.

Chuck Gallozzi
www.personal-development.com

■ Take Initiative

Leaders take initiative. Successful people take initiative. If you think of any accomplishment, world-renowned or personal, it all started with someone taking initiative. Taking initiative, regardless of how small the task, sends a signal to all that you're a "go-getter."

> Being proactive is more than taking initiative. It is recognizing that we are responsible for our own choices and have the freedom to choose based on principles and values rather than on moods or condition. Proactive people are agents of change and choose not to be victims, to be reactive, or to blame others.
>
> — *Stephen Covey*

This behavior sets you apart from the majority and will demand respect from everyone who notices." Go-getters" are usually high achievers, and their drive comes from within. Having this quality already means you are well on your way to greatness.

So why do people lack initiative? Taking initiative can be hard, but it does not have to be. When you look at initiative, the hesitation usually boils down to a couple of areas. Below are some common causes and suggested strategies for powering through the challenges.

Fear

Fear holds us back and is a great motivator that prevents us from reaching our goals. Fear of failure. Fear of rejection. Fear of loss. Fear of pain. These are all common fears that keep us from taking initiative. I once had a fear of rollercoasters. This kept me from participating in various activities at the amusement park. Then, one day, I went with a friend to get on a roller coaster, just like that. I stood in line, got a pep talk, got on and took the ride.

Strategy: I didn't know it at the time, but I had applied the understanding that fear is simply an emotion, and I instantly changed my fear emotion with an excitement emotion. Instead of being afraid of what disaster could happen I focused instead on the excitement of the thrill and rush from the ride. I applied this strategy on a massive level, but it can be applied at any level. By translating your fear into something positive and motivating, you can start the initiative quickly.

Rather than being afraid to make that tough phone call, translate that fear into an empowering emotion like accomplishment.

> Define some reasons why people don't take initiative?

Knowledge

Sometimes, we fail to take initiative because we lack the knowledge or talent to accomplish something. Sometimes this is an absolute lack of knowledge, perceived; sometimes it just doesn't matter.

Strategy: Can you learn it, and if so, how quickly? Can you leverage the task to someone with the skill you lack?

Timing

Often, we wait for the "right" time to take initiative—tomorrow, next week, next year. But when we're honest with ourselves, we know that tomorrow never comes until we take initiative. Timing is important. You don't want to rush an important decision, conversation, or project. However, don't let a good time pass waiting for the "perfect" time.

Strategy: Moving from failure to success is easier than moving from excuses to success. It does not hurt to envision the perfect scenario when setting out on a path. Add an exemplary scenario, including the timing, and seize the opportunity

> Taken initiative pays off. It is hard to visualize someone as a leader if he or she is always waiting to be told what to do.
>
> – *Sheryl Sandberg*

when "good" approaches. It may not be perfect, but at least you've started down the right path and can correct along the way.

Overwhelm

A challenge to initiative is overwhelm. Not knowing where to begin. This challenge can be a hurdle or crippling depending on the size of the task and your preparation to handle it.

Strategy: Group it and plan it. No matter how big, any task can be broken down into its elements. By grouping a significant project into big parts, then smaller parts, then individual tasks it is much easier to handle. You can also create a detailed plan on how to go about accomplishing each task along the way. In addition to a few of the strategies listed above, hiring a coach is another powerful strategy for helping kick-start your initiative. A coach can help you identify what might be holding you back, provide perspective, help you set goals, plan & prioritize, and keep you accountable for growth and success.

■ Focus

One question that often comes up from those who want to become more personally successful or stronger leaders is: What typically defines the most successful person, or how does someone lead the pack? Without hesitation, my reply is **FOCUS**.

Knowing what result you want to achieve and relentlessly pursuing its attainment is what makes people successful. The ability to maintain focus is a leadership trait.

- **Know WHAT you want to achieve each day.** If you arise each day with a set of goals that you WILL achieve before the end of the day, you are ahead of most. This is not a list of "ought to" but rather a list of "WILL DO".

- **Attach a meaning to each result**. What will achieving the result mean to you? This will help you maintain your focus throughout the day. Give the meaning some sizzle. Because the boss wants me to, it is motivating to some degree, but that can keep you in fear or distracted by the potential outcome of failing to achieve. Make the meaning personal and something that can get you fired up!

- **Create a system for success**. In basketball, players are coached during practice to shoot a free throw the exact same way each time. Whatever it is - bounce the ball three times, spin it in your hands, deep breath, shoot. It doesn't matter, but you have to do it the same way every time. Why? Because when you get in a game with pressure coming at you from fans you can settle down, go into your rhythm and shoot the easy shot. The same is true for you at work. Know how you work best and how you want your day to unfold. Then plan it out ahead of time and execute.

- **Say NO. Or at least set expectations.** Everyone in today's busy workplace has many tasks and demands. If you are to be focused, you either need to say "no" to new demands or set expectations that allow you to under promise and overdeliver. The expectation should be set to allow you to achieve the goals you are focused on first, and then take on the new items. You will need to prioritize when there is a critical and urgent situation, but don't let everything be vital and urgent

FOCUS. I believe that if you have no other trait than focus, you will find success in your life. With focus, you create the tools and gain the knowledge you need to achieve desired results.

TAKE ACTION NOW!
- Think of the one important action you must take within 24 hours. Write it down
- Why do you **want** to achieve it? Make your "why" meaningful to YOU.
- What obstacle(s) might get in your way (other people's demands, distractions)? How can you overcome those obstacles? How can you effectively set others' expectations so you can reach your goal?
- Share this action and your "why" with your leadership coach (or other personal accountability partner) now

It allows forgoing immediate satisfaction in order to gain something better, but it requires effort and time.

■ Being Disciplined

Of all the qualities, this is perhaps the most used and oftentimes can be the most difficult.

According to Author/Todd Smith, self-discipline is a pattern of behavior where you choose to do what you know you should do, rather than what you want to do. It's the inner power that pushes you to get out of bed to exercise rather than sleeping in. It is the assertion of willpower over more basic desires and is synonymous with self-control. It includes having the personal initiative to get started and the stamina to persevere. Being disciplined gives you the strength to withstand hardships and difficulties, whether physical, emotional or mental.

Discipline is one of the cornerstones of a successful and fulfilling life, and we should all strive to master it.

Benefits of becoming a disciplined person

When you are consistent in doing the things you know you should do, **when** you know you should do them, here are the benefits you will enjoy:

- You will achieve your goals. When you consistently do what you know you should do, your odds of achieving your goals will be dramatically increased.

- You self-esteem will soar. Every time you push yourself to do something you know you should do, you are building your self-esteem.

- People's respect for you will grow. This includes everyone from your spouse to your employer who witnesses your efforts.

Define Discipline?

- You will influence the lives of others. Every good and right thing you do influences the lives of those who are watching and can have a ripple effect on future generations.

- You will see greater success in all areas of your life. Jim Rohn said, *"For every disciplined effort there is a multiple return."* Think about it.

- You will enjoy a more rewarding and satisfying life.

Downside of lacking discipline

When you consistently neglect to do the things you know you should do, **when** they should be done, here's the downside:

- You won't achieve your goals. I've never met anyone who achieved any worthwhile goal who lacked discipline.

- You won't feel good about yourself. No matter how hard you try to justify your actions, you know what's right and wrong. Lying to yourself only makes it worse.

- You'll lose the respect of those who are dependent upon your actions.

Making the decision to become a disciplined person may prove to be one of the most important decisions you make because of its powerful influence on every part of your life.

A commitment to discipline
The first step in becoming a disciplined person is to make a commitment to yourself that from this day forward, you are going to do the things you know you should do, when you should do them. As part of this commitment, you cannot allow yourself to make excuses or justify not doing what you should do.

If you struggle with discipline, start small. It's how we all got started. Start by taking out the overflowing garbage, answering an email, changing the light bulb, or cleaning your bathroom. Start today doing all the little things you know you should do, but don't feel like doing.

When you need to do things that make you uncomfortable, remember the wise words of leadership expert Dr. John Maxwell who said, "If we're growing, we're always going to be out of our comfort zone."

When things come up that are scary, heed the experience of Dale Carnegie who said, *"Do the thing you fear to do and keep on doing it... that is the quickest and surest way ever yet discovered to conquer fear."*

Becoming a disciplined person will likely be the hardest thing you do, but it can also become the most rewarding. All successes in every part of your life are built on the foundation of discipline.

I want to challenge you to start doing the little things you know you should do. As you do, recognize yourself for each thing you do. With constant awareness and sustained effort, you can actually train yourself to become disciplined.

Discipline is one of the key differentiators separating those who live successful and fulfilling lives from those who don't.

■ Don't Complain

Work isn't perfect, but if you are <u>lucky enough to have a job</u> right now it pays to remember that millions and millions of Americans don't think you have a thing to complain about. So why are so many people complaining?

I have come to realize that people who complain do it because it's what they do. It doesn't matter what the circumstance is, if you improve the condition in one area, they'll start complaining about another.

According to the U.S. Bureau of Labor Statistics, the nation's unemployment rate is hovering around 10%. Even more troubling, *The New York Times* reports that <u>unemployed people</u> are spending longer periods between jobs.

Leaders in all professions do not like complainers. Because that kind of chronic complaining, justified or not, in the workplace leads to no good. In fact, in can be downright toxic and can make a department or even a whole company a terrible place to work.

Here's why constant complaining is so bad:

1: It makes things look worse than they are
When people complain, they focus only on what's wrong. Things may be mostly fine in the company, but complainers only talk about the problems, annoyances, and peeves they perceive.

If things in a company are 80% good and 20% bad, and you spend most of your time thinking and talking about the bad 20%, the situation will look a lot worse than it really is.

2: It becomes a habit
The more you complain, the easier it gets. In the end, everything is bad, every situation is a problem, every co-worker is a jerk, and nothing is good.

The more you focus on the negative, the harder it gets to switch into a positive mindset.

3: You get what you focus on
According to Wikipedia, Confirmation bias is:
...a tendency to search for or interpret new information in a way that confirms one's preconceptions and avoid information and interpretations that contradict prior beliefs.

In other words, what you already believe influences your perception of everything around you. That's why constant complaining makes you see everything in a negative light, because your subconscious mind tries to make new observations fit with what you already know.

4: It leads to one-downmanship
A complaining session might go something like this:

The other day, my boss came in 5 minutes before I was leaving and asked me to finish two huge projects for him. I had to stay two hours and missed my football game.
Yeah, well, my boss told me to work this weekend AND the next.
Hah, that's nothing! My boss...
This type of interaction rewards the person with the worst story who can complain the loudest. Not healthy!

5: It makes people despondent
Not only does constant complaining make you see the workplace as worse than it really is, but because you're constantly hearing stories of how bad things are and how they're constantly getting worse, it also destroys all hope that things can get better.

This of course makes people less likely to take action to improve their situation, because everybody knows it's doomed to fail anyway.

> Identify some examples why complaining isn't good?

6: It kills innovation
Because the situation looks so hopeless, people become less creative and innovative. What's the point of coming up with ideas and implementing them – it's never going to work anyway.

Also, chronic complainers are the first to shoot down any new idea.

7: It favors negative people
The way to get status among complainers is to be the most negative. To be the one who sees everything in the most negative light.

Any attempt to be positive or cheerful will be shot down, and optimists will be accused of being Pollyannas, naive, and unrealistic.

8: It creates cliques
Being positive, optimistic and appreciative makes you more open towards other people – no matter who they are. It becomes easy to connect to co-workers in other departments, projects, or divisions.

Complaining, on the other hand, makes people gather in cliques with their fellow complainers where they can be critical and suspicious of everybody else.

> One of the most compelling reasons for choosing to not complain is that complaining does nothing to fix your problems. Regardless of what you are facing, choosing to be negative and verbalize your frustrations isn't going to help your situation.

9: Pessimism is bad for you

Psychologist Martin Seligman showed in his groundbreaking research in positive psychology that people who see the world in a positive light have a long list of advantages, including:

> ➢ They live longer
> ➢ They're healthier
> ➢ They have more friends and better social lives
> ➢ They enjoy life more
> ➢ They're more successful at work

We sometimes think that pessimists and complainers have the edge because they see problems sooner, but the truth is that optimists not only lead better lives, they're also more successful because they believe that what they're doing is going to work.

THE UPSHOT

Constant complaining in the workplace is toxic. It can drain the happiness, motivation, creativity and fun from a whole company. Wherever it's going on it must be addressed and handled properly.

I'm NOT saying that we should never complain at work – quite the contrary. If you see a problem in your workplace, complain to whoever can do something about it. What we should avoid at all costs, is constant bitching and moaning, where we're always complaining about the same things, to the same people, in the same way, day in and day out.

So what can we do about it? Well, first of all, each of us can learn to complain constructively. This means learning to complain in a way that leads to the problem being fixed – rather than to more complaining.

Secondly, we can learn to deal with the chronic complainers we meet at work. Unfortunately, our traditional strategies, like trying to cheer them up or suggesting solutions for their problems, don't work because complainers aren't looking for encouragement or solutions. Here's my post on how to deal with chronic complainers.

Finally, you can train your own ability to be positive. Just like complaining can become a habit, so can being appreciative, optimistic, and grateful. You could declare today a positive day, you could take a few minutes at the end of every work day to write down five good experiences from that day or you could praise a co-worker.   - Alexander Kjerulf

■ Have Good Communication and Customer Service Skills

All jobs require good customer service skills in some form or fashion, but especially if in constant communication with internal and external customers. Besides deterrence, Security Officers main areas of focus will be provide direction, signing in/out visitors and guests, enforce policies and procedures, calm abusive behavior, and working as a team. All of which require excellent communication and customer service and some more than others.

Over 90% of all security jobs require this ability, but depending on the post, it will dictate the *amount of customer service actually needed.* In some instances, where the security of products or services, people, or procedures will demand the utmost security consciousness, customer service will not be the main objective, but still needed, and hiring Managers must understand the difference before bringing newly hired officers onto the scene.

This ability is one that if you have it, can quickly tip the scale in your favor and is one of the broadest skills used while working in the Security industry.

From my experience, most people like to think they are customer service-oriented. But I have found that when put in front of customers, or when certain situations occur, they're clearly lacking. There are tons of reasons why this happens, but these are the ones I have witnessed more than others. They are:

> - when a procedure becomes repetitive,
> - when something doesn't go as planned,
> - when a desired result isn't achieved, and
> - when given constructive criticism.

The truth is it takes a special type of person along with maturity to have great customer service skills. While this certainly isn't the job for the meek, it can be developed with the right training. The constant interaction with the diversity of people will be the ultimate test. This skill will prove invaluable and one that you must have if you want to achieve success.

■ Have Good Judgment

Just as the Law and the Constitution provide Police Officers with responsibilities, so do Post Orders, Site Policy and Procedures manuals for Security officers. However, not everything is written in black and white. Good judgment and common sense should always be part of the job no matter where a security officer is employed.

As discussed in *"Client Expectations,"* good judgment comes from experience. And experience usually comes from "bad" judgment. Although a lot of mistakes are learned by trial and error, it is neither the only nor the best way of learning, but from other people's experiences.

You ever notice some people seem to never get into trouble and go on having a very productive lifestyle, while others constantly get in and out of trouble and don't seem to know why or fail to acknowledge it. It all goes back to judgment.

A security officer should be rational and practical enough to make judgment calls. The ability to make good judgment decisions is essential in dealing with sensitive situations. It can mean the difference between getting disciplined or being promoted, as well as life or death in certain situations. Therefore, he/she should be able to sense the intensity of the problem and tackle an unprecedented situation properly. Having good judgment is a major component of success or failure in our personal and professional lives.

With good judgment, the possibilities are endless. It is the one trait constantly being exercised even when we're not aware of it.
Unless we don't have the capabilities, every decision we make or do in our entire life is a judgment call. Our present and future will be the result of these judgments.

None of us has exercised good judgment all the time. We can all look back on past circumstances and wish we had acted differently.

A lot of judgment will often involve split decision-making at a moment's notice and although we may not think about it then, pausing and thinking before acting will eliminate a lot of bad choices.

The following questions are designed to aid in your thinking process before making a decision. While performing your job, if you ask yourself these questions *before*, you will be more equipped to make better judgment decisions while choosing to act or not. They are:

1. How will my actions affect someone else if I do this
2. Depending on the situation, how will the outcome benefit me, the person, or the company
3. What would someone else do if they were in this situation
4. How will I be looked at if I did/or didn't do something

5. Learn from other people's mistakes

In security it helps to always maintain perspective of why you are there in the first place - security of people, products or services.

■ Thought Process when Performing Mundane Duties

Security Officers will likely have some duties and responsibilities that may appear to be performed for no apparent rhyme or reason, from the officer's perspective. Like securing an empty facility, or making rounds in areas with no potential threat of violence or potential harm whatsoever. And they may be correct. But what's not often realized is that *someone* has a stake in the claim of the property or facility that, in their opinion, warrants securing.

Although not always the case, officers should understand the nature of why duties are performed. The importance of this cannot be overstated. Knowing the meaning of carrying out a particular task gives meaning to its nature and provides the necessary impact of its significance. If security officers have not been informed, they should ask. If put in these situations, do not feel embarrassed or ashamed to ask, and when you do, do so in a respectable manner. In most cases, your Supervisor and/or Manager of the account will know and provide this information. This answer may also be provided in a Policy or post-procedures manual. Just like any job, your performance must still be to the utmost satisfaction regardless of its perceived importance.

As Security professionals, your level of commitment must not be dictated by the job's importance to you, but remain constant. Your Security Company and the client will also expect officers to be committed and perform all duties in a very professional, dedicated, and respectful manner.

SUMMARY

- Just because someone else thinks you are ready for a security position doesn't mean you are.

- How you feel about yourself has the most significant impact on how you view others.

- Without confidence in yourself, it will be hard to get others to have confidence in you.

- Being a Security Officer requires the following characteristics.

  - Being able to set a good example for the team
  - keeping your personal feelings from getting in the way of performing your job
  - disciplined in doing what's needed
  - knowing how to receive constructive criticism
  - handling pressure
  - being a team player and learning how to fit in
  - being an effective communicator

- What makes a good security officer will largely depend on their willingness to adapt and ability to develop the new skills needed for the position.

CHAPTER 9
SAMPLE INTERVIEW QUESTIONNAIRE AND GENERAL KNOWLEDGE EXAMINATION

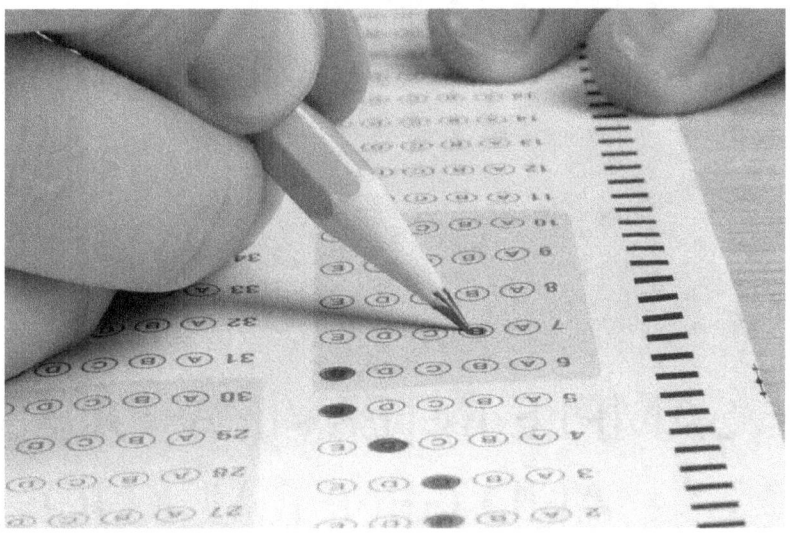

SAMPLE INTERVIEW QUESTIONNAIRE AND GENERAL KNOWLEDGE EXAMINATION

CHAPTER 9
SAMPLE INTERVIEW QUESTIONNAIRE AND GENERAL KNOWLEDGE EXAMINATION

Security positions are on the rise, and if you are interested, now is the opportunity. Security is looking for good people from all backgrounds, but before you apply, you need to be prepared.

In addition to some general interview questions, you will be asked job-specific questions that you will be expected to answer. These questions will assess your qualifications, skillsets, and knowledge of the position you seek. In addition to your skill sets, the hiring manager will be looking to see if you have the right mindset and ability to fit in with the current employees.

The interviewer's goal is to find the best-suited candidate for the position offered. CAN YOU DO THE JOB? When conducting job interviews, that's at the forefront of every hiring manager's mind. So when you respond, keep this in mind. Your goal is to show that you are the best fit for the job out of all the applicants the employer is interviewing.

Here are tips on how to answer the questions so you can show the interviewer that you have all the qualifications the company is seeking, according to about.com.

Check the Job Requirements. Before you go to an interview, check the job requirements listed in the job posting you responded to. Make a list of the skills you have that match those requirements. Review the list prior to the interview, and if you need a "cheat sheet," jot down the list on the notepad that you bring to the interview with you.

Show What You Know. Show the interviewer that you know how to do the job by giving specific examples of the knowledge you have when responding to interview questions. When you respond with actual on-the-job experiences and situations you have encountered at work, you're showing the interviewer what you know instead of just saying you can do the job.

Showcase Your Skills. As I mentioned, the company has a specific skill set in mind. That's why you were selected for an interview. The skills you listed on your resume and mentioned in your cover letter got you the interview. Be sure that you know exactly what's on your resume or CV and what you entered if you filled out a job application. Highlight the most relevant skills during your interview.

Capitalize on Credentials. Do you have a degree, or have you taken coursework in the field? Do you have certifications or special training for the job? Be sure to mention your credentials during the interview. Knowledge really is power when it comes to job interviews, and the more you can relay what you know, the better chance you will have of being invited for a <u>second interview</u> and ultimately getting a job offer.

Be Honest. Regardless of how much you want the job, be honest and don't say you know how to do something if you don't. If you don't have all the required skills or educational requirements, the company may be willing to train you. If not, the job isn't going to be a good fit, and it's going to be a challenge to succeed in the role at the company. It's better to pass on a job than it is to fail and end up losing it because you weren't qualified.

■ Interview Questions

The interview is a big part of the job-search process. Now that you have an interview, there are certain things you will want to do in advance to prepare for it. The more you prepare, the more relaxed you'll feel. Another way to get ready for the big day is to anticipate what kinds of questions you'll be asked and work out your responses in advance

Remember, your job is to convince the recruiter/hiring manager that you have the skills, knowledge, and experience for the job. It also shows the employer what you can do for the company, and it gives you an opportunity to assess whether your qualifications and career ambitions align with the position. Show motivation and convince him/her that you fit the organization's culture and job description, and you get that much closer to an offer.

Here are some <u>general and job-specific questions.</u>. Consider how you might answer them before you get face-to-face.

1. So...tell me about yourself?

2. Your application lists quite a few jobs; what will this job offer that others did not?

3. If I were to contact your previous boss, what would they tell me about you?

4. As Security Professionals, we often work when others do not. How do you feel about that?

5. Why do you want to be a Security Professional?

6. What are some of your weaknesses?

7. There are several gaps in your employment history. Can you explain them?

8. Why do you want to leave your current position?

9. Give me an example of a problem you faced on the job, and how you solved it.

10. Have you ever had a problem with a former Supervisor or Manager? If so, describe the situation and what the outcome was.

11. Do you consider yourself to be a team player?

12. Where do you see yourself in 5 years?

13. Do you have any experience in reacting to emergency situations? If so, explain.

14. Do you enjoy helping others? If so, give me an example that required you to assist when you did not have to?

Manager interviewing applicant

15. Have you ever been fired from a job, and/or received any form of disciplinary?

16. Can you describe a scenario when you have had to resolve a conflict with someone who disagreed with you?

17. In your opinion, what does success mean to you?

18. How do you think a friend or teacher would describe you?

19. What challenges do you see if you were hired for this position?

20. What have you learned from your previous mistakes?

21. What did you like the least and best about your previous job?

22. In your own words, what does customer service mean to you?

23. What qualifications or experience do you have that can relate to our role here?

24. There's usually stress on the job, and everyone copes in their own measure. Has there been a time when you were faced with stress or a problem that tested your coping abilities, and how did you handle it?

25. Can you recall the worst mistake you ever made while working?

26. Why should I hire you? Others are waiting for employment - what will you bring that they cannot?

27. Tell me about when you had to conform to a policy you disagreed with. What was the outcome?

■ Examination

If you are serious about becoming a Security Officer, you should have obtained certain knowledge while continually striving for improvements. Let's test your knowledge below and see if you are ready to become one.

1. The _____determines the style of uniform many Security Officers wear on-site.

   a. Security Company
   b. Security Officer
   c. Client
   d. Officers parents

2. **Yes or No**
   A civilian jacket can be worn with your uniform.

3. **True or False**
   Extreme hair styles and flamboyant colors are not authorized while performing security-related duties.

4. **Why is maintaining a neat and professional uniform appearance important?**
   _____
   _____

5. **True or False:**
   Are all Security Officers required to be licensed?

6. **You are an employee of a department store and perform security functions. You are classified as a _____ Security Officer.**

7. **While patrolling the perimeter, several lights are burned out above the employee entranceway. You should _____.**

   a. Report it to your Supervisor
   b. Create an Incident Report
   c. Do nothing, it's the Company's responsibility
   d. Make a note and inform the Janitor whenever you see him

8. **You just woke up and realized you will be running about 30 minutes late for duty. What is the first thing you should do?**

   a. Get to work as fast as you can
   b. Call off, you don't want to be late
   c. Notify your Supervisor and/or appropriate personnel
   d. Get dressed

9. **You would like to attend a wedding tomorrow and would like to be excused from work. After informing your supervisor, she explained she cannot afford to give you off. What should you do?**

   a. Put in a time-off request form
   b. Report to work as scheduled
   c. Have another employee work for you if they agree
   d. Call off, the post will then get covered by someone else

10. **You are in the Patrol vehicle and have just been informed of a vehicle accident on the property. The accident is about 300 meters away, and the posted speed limit is 15mph. You are in the middle of your patrol rounds and will be finished in about 10 minutes. You should:**

  a. Stop your rounds and drive safely to the accident as fast as you can.
  b. Immediately respond, but obey the posted speed limit.
  c. Turn your overhead lights on and put the pedal to the medal. Everyone else will move out your way.
  d. Complete your rounds and then respond to the accident as soon as possible.

11. Yes or No:
Your shift just ended, but your relief has not arrived. It's okay to leave, but ensure that you annotate your relief status on the paperwork (DAR).

12. True or False:
You can be terminated if it is found that you knew of a policy violation without disclosing it?

13. Officer Jasmine usually works day shift but is working 2nd shift due to a call-off. While performing her duties, the Supervisor notices an incorrect procedure and instructs her on the correct way. After the Supervisor leaves, Officer Jasmine should:

  a. Continue doing it the way she was trained
  b. Do as the Supervisor instructs her
  c. Inform the Supervisor that she doesn't work his shift
  d. Ask to switch posts with another officer

14. In the Security Industry, the two types of customers are _____ and _____.

  a. Satisfied and Dissatisfied
  b. Internal and External
  c. Clients and co-workers

15. You are working a post that requires you to check all vehicles before entry and departure. You notice the Client is about to depart for the second time, you should:

  a. Disregard checking the Client; he was checked earlier.
  b. Notify your Supervisor for further instructions.
  c. Follow the procedure and check his vehicle.
  d. Check his vehicle, but not as you usually would if it were everyone else.

16. Yes or No:
While performing your duties, you accidentally slipped on a wet surface but did not get injured. Should you report the work accident?

17. State-issued Security Guard licenses are valid for _____ year(s).
    a. 1   b. 2   c.3   d. No license is required

18. What is the difference between a full-time and a temporary employee?
    _____
    _____

19. After checking your pockets, you left work 30 minutes ago and realized you forgot to turn over the keys. There are spare keys available on-site. You should:

    a. Immediately turn around and take them back
    b. Bring them in tomorrow when you work
    c. Call the on-duty supervisor and inform him of the mistake; take instructions from him
    d. You can discard them, they have spares

20. What is the purpose of DCJS?

    a. Regulates the licensing requirement for Security Officers.
    b. Regulates the licensing requirements for Police Officers.
    c. Reporting agency for security call-offs
    d. Ensure all security locations have a set of post orders

21. While performing your duty, a customer gets irate and calls you by name. How should you respond?

    a. Return the favor
    b. Have someone else deal with the customer.
    c. Stay calm and complete the transaction. After that, report abuse through your chain of command.
    d. Remember you are in a position of authority. Use scare tactics and get the job done.

22. True or False
    The Security Company automatically pays for jury duty leave.

23. Which of the following may be grounds for termination

    a. Sleeping on duty
    b. Failure to follow the instructions of the Supervisor
    c. Violation of policy or procedure
    d. All of the above

24. **You discover that your Supervisor has installed "Candy Crush", your favorite game, on his computer. It's 2:00 am in the morning, and you are bored. You know his computer password. What should you do?**

    a. Delete the game
    b. Play the game, but ask the Supervisor
    c. Report the Supervisor to your next level Manager
    d. Play the game for no more than 1 hour

25. **Becoming a Security Officer means you will play a vital role in ensuring clients' safety and security of people, products, and _____.**

26. **When reporting for duty, you should arrive at your job site about _____minutes early.**

    a. 5
    b. 10
    c. 15
    d. As long as you are on time

27. **The main responsibility of the _____ positions is access control, and only authorized and approved personnel will be granted permission to pass through.**

    a. Interior Patrol
    b. Account Manager
    c. Truck Gate/Loading Dock
    d. Customer Protection Officer

28. **True or False**
    Security Officer training varies from State to State.

29. **True or False**
    Paying employees unbilled overtime is good for Security Companies.

30. **Clients expect Security Officers to look professional, be adequately trained, have good customer service skills, and _____ and _____.**

    a. Good judgment and follow directions
    b. Leadership and communication skills
    c. Excellent driving record and telephone etiquette

31. Private security firms represent the _____, while the police represent the city, county, or state they work in.

    a. public
    b. property owners
    c. security company
    d. government

32. Security Officer wages are based on the Clients' _____.

33. You notice one of your co-workers engaged in inappropriate behavior with a customer. You should:

    a. Keep it to yourself since no one will find out
    b. Join in
    c. Inform co-worker of inappropriate behavior
    d. Inform co-worker and then your on-duty Supervisor

34. You notice customers smoking in an unauthorized area while performing your duties. Your shift ends in 20 minutes, and you still have remaining duties that need to get done. You should:

    a. Enforce the policy and have them move to an authorized area
    b. notify your Supervisor
    c. Continue with your rounds. If time permits, enforce the policy afterwards.
    d. nothing, no harm is being done, and no one is hurt

35. Yes or No:
While working an isolated post driving a patrol vehicle, your girlfriend shows up and asks if she can ride along. You looked for instructions regarding picking up passengers but could not find any. Is it okay to let her ride along for a few minutes?

36. When would it be okay to disobey a policy or procedure?

    a. Only if it poses a serious health or safety hazard
    b. Never, it's there for a reason
    c. When you don't feel up to it
    d. After seeing others do it

37. You need to speak with your Supervisor regarding an issue and go to confront him. When you walk in, she's in the control room with a few co-workers. You

    a. Wait until he gets off

  b. Ask to speak with her in private
  c. Start addressing the issue since others may have some concerns as well
  d. Wait and see if the issue goes away

38. Which of the following will warrant an Incident Report completed?

  a. Damage property found
  b. Medical emergency
  c. Suspicious person
  d. All of the above

39. Safety is the responsibility of _____.

  a. Supervisors
  b. Account Managers
  c. Everyone
  d. Clients

40. Yes or No:
Can an employee take paid vacation if they have not worked long enough to earn any?

41. True or False:
Officers working Holidays receive 2 times their regular pay rate?

42. Being _____ means being responsive to change and being adaptable to new ideas or conditions.

  a. committed
  b. customer-oriented
  c. cautious
  d. flexible

43. As a Security Officer, your_____ will have the biggest impact on how others see and ultimately treat you.

  a. co-workers
  b. appearance
  c. facial expression
  d. skillset

44. To improve your chances of being promoted, you should do the following:

  a. Look professional and take initiative

b. Have a winning attitude and be flexible
c. Stop making excuses and stay focused
d. Be disciplined and stop complaining
e. All of the above

45. True or False:
Having good judgment skills is not a requirement for a Security Officer.

46. True or False:
Professionalism isn't what you do, but how you do it.

47. True or False:
Since Security Officers work for property owners, codes and ethics are not required.

48. _____ are the most valuable assets of Security Providers.

a. Security Officers
b. Clients
c. Company managers
d. public

49. True or False:
Annual promotions are automatic on all security contracts.

50. True or False:
Clients have the authority to request the removal of a Security Officer from working their contract at any time.

This concludes the
SECURITY PROFESSIONAL

By now, you should be armed with the information, knowledgeable of the duties, and prepared for the expectations. You should clearly understand the responsibility and dedication needed to become a security professional. I hope you have enjoyed the material, learned what's expected, and will put the information to use. If so, it will significantly enhance your chances of becoming a professional and provide the necessary skills needed to enhance professionalism in the security industry. Not only will this benefit you, but also the Company, co-workers, customers, and everyone you come in contact with.

Thank you, and God bless.

Roy Wyatt

Exam Answer Sheet
Basic Security Officer Examination

1. c
2. No
3. True
4. Not only is this a requirement, but your uniform will determine others outlook of you
5. False
6. "In-house" Security Officer
7. a
8. c
9. b
10. a
11. No
12. True
13. b
14. b
15. c
16. Yes
17. b
18. <u>Temporary</u> – employees hired for a specific period of time
    <u>Full-time</u> – employees scheduled to work full-time hours as deemed by company.
19. c
20. a
21. c
22. False
23. d
24. c
25. Services
26. c
27. c
28. True
29. False
30. a
31. b
32. Bill rates
33. d
34. a

35. No
36. a
37. b

38. d

39. c
40. No
41. False
42. d
43. b
44. e
45. False
46. True
47. False
48. a
49. False

50. True

CONCLUSION

The Security Professional has presented a great deal of information in the hope of better educating the Security personnel on the standards and expectations needed to become a Professional Security Officer.

The information presented should indicate that the Private Security Industry continues to experience rapid growth and changes. Unfortunately, for most Private Security Officers, this growth and change have not resulted in higher living standards. Meager wages and few benefits still plague Security Officers, especially those employed in contract security. Since most companies are contracting out security, employment in Petty security will continue to decline in the years to come.

So what does this mean for the Security Officer?

No one knows for certain the answer to that question. But what is known is that the demand for private security will continue to rise, which will lead to the need for better-qualified and trained Officers... professionals.

Having said that, there are plenty of careers in the Security Industry with wages compatible with the job market, but you must be prepared. If you desire to achieve more, it's there for the taking, and it's totally up to you.

I hope any Security Officer reading this will take this newfound knowledge, evaluate his or her life, and ask where he/she want to be in the next year, two, five, or ten years from now in regard to a career.

"The quality of a person's life is in direct proportion to their commitment to excellence, regardless of their chosen field of endeavor."
_Vincent T. Lombardi

If you want to improve your life, you must invest in yourself. Pursuing education or obtaining a degree will prepare you for a better position in the security industry.

Simply complaining that wages and benefits provided by an employer are not enough or are unsatisfactory is not a viable excuse. Security personnel who are not satisfied with their job and/or career must decide to improve themselves for no other reason than to benefit themselves.

The Security Industry has always been and will always be the face of many professions. The continued rise in employment will guarantee a security blanket for many Officers who are willing to put forth the effort to become what this industry demands: professionals. Anyone looking to get into the Industry needs to understand its complexities and be prepared for its increasing and ever-changing demands.

If you are, the power is in your hands. You hold the key to your future. If you desire to succeed in the security industry, nothing is holding you back except yourself. This booklet was written as a reminder and tool for anyone wanting advancement and gaining knowledge of what the industry needs. Where you go from here is up to you.

www.ingramcontent.com/pod-product-compliance
Lightning Source LLC
Chambersburg PA
CBHW062350220526
45472CB00008B/1762